NEXUS
TOEFL®
*i*BT

Listening

Starter

성공적인 학습을 위한 단계별 전략!
Development & Progress for Completion
NEXUS TOEFL *i*BT Listening Starter

지은이 넥서스영어교육연구소, Kerry Williamson,
        Virginia Hanslien, Mary French
펴낸이 임상진
펴낸곳 (주)넥서스

출판신고 1992년 4월 3일 제311-2002-2호 ㉓
10880 경기도 파주시 지목로 5
Tel (02)330-5500 Fax (02)330-5555

ISBN   978-89-6000-625-6   54740

www.nexusEDU.kr
NEXUS Edu는 넥서스의 초·중·고 학습물 전문 브랜드입니다.

성공적인 학습을 위한 단계별 전략!
Development & Progress for Completion

NEXUS
TOEFL® iBT

Listening

Starter

NEXUS Edu

머리말

영어를 배우는 데 있어서, 네 가지 언어 영역을 균형 있게 학습해야 할 필요성은 오랫동안 인지되어 왔다. 하지만 국내 영어 학습 현실 속에서 그런 학습을 진행하기에는 현실적 여건이 따라 주질 못했다. 먼저 말하기나 쓰기 부분의 공인된 평가가 많지 않았던 탓도 있겠지만, 현실적으로 수업시간에 활용할 수 있는 다양한 학습 모델이 많지 않았기 때문이기도 하다.

그러나 CBT 토플이 *i*BT로 바뀌어 speaking과 writing이 새롭게 추가되면서 여러 변화가 생겼다. 전반적인 문제 유형이 일차원적 문제 풀이 방식에서 벗어나 제공되는 정보를 잘 정리하여 이해하고, 이해한 내용을 다시 정리하여 표현할 수 있는 능력이 더 중요하게 되었다. 이런 능력 향상은 영어를 배울 때 암기와 반복에 의존하는 학습 방식보다는 절제된 문장 구조 속에서 "organized thoughts"를 할 수 있도록 유도하는 학습 방식을 통해 더 효과적으로 향상될 수 있다. 말하기나 쓰기의 통합적인 영역에서만 이런 능력이 필요한 것이 아니라, 독해 및 청취 영역에서도 마찬가지이다. 문제에 근거한 내용만을 맞히는 것이 아니라, 문단 간의 정보 관계를 전체적으로(global understanding) 훑을 수 있는 훈련이 되어야 한다. 따라서 토플을 단기간에 한 권으로 끝을 내려한다거나 한 학기의 강의 수업 방식으로 짧은 시간에 높은 성적을 올리기에 급급하기보다는 위와 같은 학습 방식에 초점을 맞춰 체계적인 계획을 가지고 접근하게 되면, 토플 성적 이외에도 전반적인 영어 실력을 키워갈 수 있으리라 생각된다.

넥서스 토플은 전반적으로 위와 같은 취지로 기획되었다. 다시 말해, 각 단원마다 주어진 스킬만 배우고 끝내는 것이 아니라 앞서 학습한 스킬을 다시 반복학습할 수 있게 하고, 지문을 통합적으로 활용하며, 짧은 시간 안에 정보의 구조를 파악하는 능력을 훈련할 수 있도록 구성하였다.

짧은 시간에 점수를 올리려는 전략적인 학습 방식을 선호하기보다는 체계적인 학습 계획과 그에 맞는 적절한 교재를 활용하여 토플 점수 향상 이외에도 영어로 생각하고 정리하는 표현 기술을 잘 연마할 수 있도록 학습하는 데 있어 이 교재가 많은 도움이 되기를 바란다.

| 넥서스영어교육연구소 |

이 책의 특징

1 단계별 기본 학습 훈련 장치 강조

- Second listening, Organization tree 등을 통해 청취 지문을 효과적으로 들을 수 있게 도와 주는 기본 훈련 장치를 구성하였다.

2 다양한 테마의 강의와 대화 지문 구조의 체계적 분석

- 다양한 주제의 강의와 대화를 들려 주고, 그 구조를 체계적으로 분석할 수 있는 activity를 마련하였다.

3 체계적인 학습 스킬과 전략 구성

- 새롭게 바뀌는 iBT Listening Section에서 나오는 질문 유형을 철저히 분석하고, 질문 유형이 요구하는 기본적인 strategies를 바탕으로 listening skill을 체계적으로 습득할 수 있도록 구성하였다.

4 어휘력 확장의 학습

- 토플에 자주 쓰이는 테마와 관련된 기본 어휘 학습을 강조하여, 어휘 능력 향상을 도모하였다.

5 iBT 실전에 맞춘 단계별 연습

- Skill Check-up, Exercise, Final Test로 이어지는 단계별 연습으로 iBT Listening에 충분히 대비할 수 있도록 구성하였다.

이 책의 구성

Overview & Sample

Overview에서는 해당 Chapter에서 학습할 질문 유형을 미리 알아 두기 위하여 전체적인 개관, Question Types, General Strategies 등을 소개하고 있다. Sample 테스트를 통해 어떤 Skill들을 학습하게 될지 해당 문제 유형을 미리보기 한다.

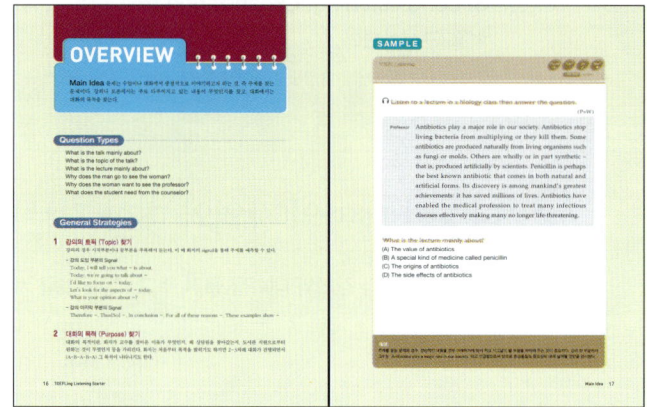

Skill Check-up

Overview에서 정리한 전략을 바탕으로 구체적인 문제유형에 맞는 Skill을 학습할 수 있다. 또한 Organization Tree를 통해 지문의 구조를 파악하여 핵심 사항들을 note-taking할 수 있는 기술을 훈련하도록 구성하였다. 여기서는 Dictation과 어휘 등 듣기와 관련한 다양한 단계별 학습이 가능하다.

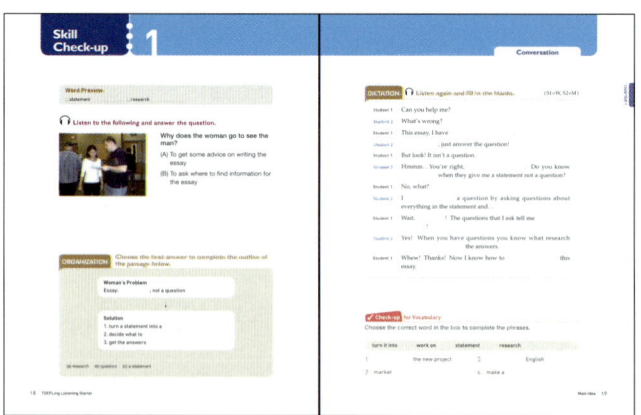

Exercise

해당 Chapter에서 학습한 질문 유형을 중점적으로 물어 본다. 다시 듣고 Note-taking을 완성하도록 하는 훈련을 통해 긴 지문을 효과적으로 정리하는 습관을 갖도록 구성하였다.

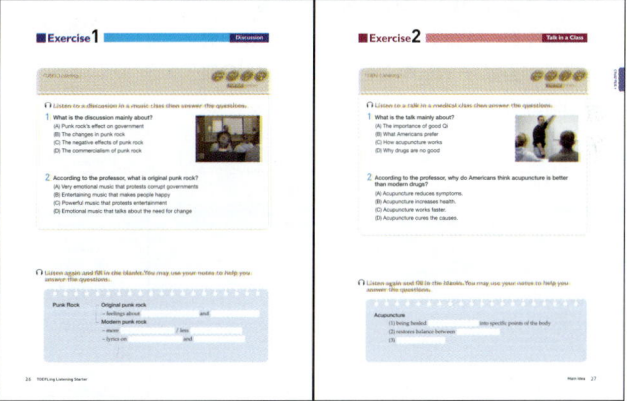

Dictation

Exercise의 스크립트를 들으면서 Dictation 연습을 해볼 수 있는 코너를 따로 마련하였다. 하단 부분에서는 지문 이해에 도움이 되도록 주요 구문을 정리하여 학습에 도움이 되도록 하였다.

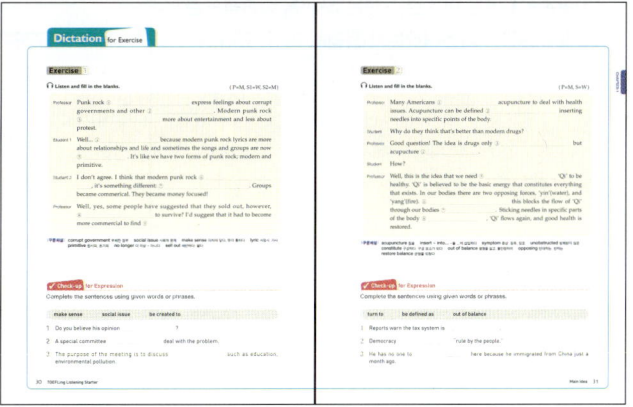

Vocabulary Review

앞에서 배운 단어들을 토대로 중요 단어 및
숙어들을 정리하였다. 학생들이 직접 자신의 어휘
실력을 점검할 수 있도록 간단한 테스트 형식으로
구성되어 있다.

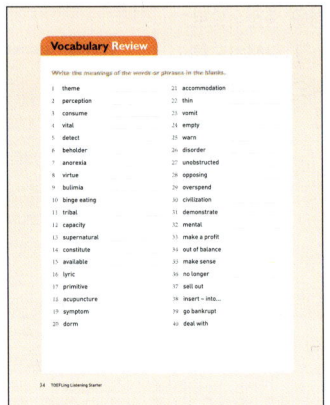

Final Test

Chapter 1~6을 아우르는 모든 Skill을 종합적으로
평가해 Skill을 마스터했는지 점검해 볼 수 있다.

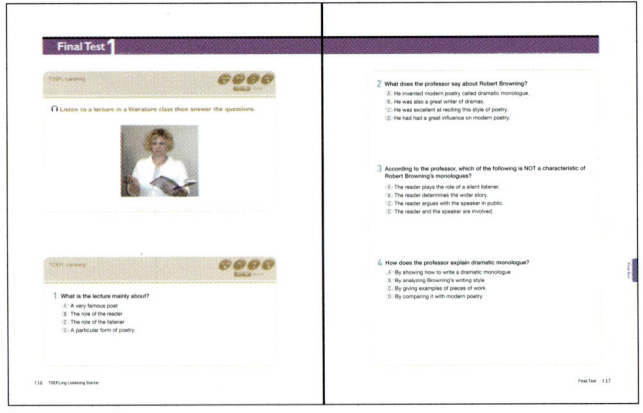

목차

Introduction to *i*BT TOEFL

Introduction to *i*BT TOEFL

*i*BT(Internet–based Test) TOEFL이란?

*i*BT는 Internet-based Test의 약자로 인터넷을 통해 시험을 치르게 하는 차세대 토플이다. 기존의 CBT가 미국으로 유학 오는 외국 학생들의 실제 영어구사능력을 제대로 측정하지 못한다는 비판에 대한 대안으로 새롭게 만들어졌으며 특히 말하기 능력에 대한 평가를 요구하는 미국 대학들의 요청에 따라 Speaking Section을 신설했다. 기존 CBT와는 달리 언어영역간의 통합을 접목시킨 것이 특징이며 학생들이 얼마나 빠르게, 제대로 미국 대학 생활에 적응해 갈 수 있을지에 대한 지표를 대학에 제공해 준다.

미국에서는 2005년 9월부터 시작되었고, 한국에서는 2006년 6월부터 실시되며, *i*BT가 실시되면 기존의 CBT 방식으로는 더 이상 시험이 치러지지 않는다.

CBT에서 *i*BT는 어떻게 달라졌나?

	CBT	*i*BT
Skills Test	Reading Listening Grammar * Writing은 별도	Reading Listening Writing Speaking
Test time	3.5 hours	4 hours
Reading	4~5 지문 (250~350 words) 각 지문당 11개 문제 (시간 70~90분)	3~5 지문 (700 words) 각 지문당 12~14개 문제 (시간 60~100 분)
Listening	1. 11~17개 대화 　　(각 지문당 1개의 질문) 2. 2~3개 짧은 대화 　　(각 지문당 2~3개의 질문) 3. 4~6개 미니 강의와 토론 　　(각각 3~6 개 문제) (시간 40~60분)	1. 4~6개의 강의 및 교실토론 　　(각 지문당 5~6개의 질문) 2. 2~3개의 대화 　　(각 5~6개의 질문) (시간 60~100분)
Speaking	없음	1. 2개의 independent tasks 　　일반 토픽에 대한 개인의 의견 발표 2. 4개의 integrated tasks 　　읽고 들었던 것을 근거하여 말하기 (시간 20분)

Writing	**One independent task** 토픽에 대한 의견을 개진하기 (시간 30분)	**1. 1개의 integrated task** 읽고 들은 내용에 근거하여 쓰기 (20분) **2. 1개의 independent task** 토픽에 대한 의견을 개진하기 (30분)
Structure (Grammar)	20~25개의 문제 (시간 15~20분)	없음
전체 점수	300	120
피드백	점수만 제공	Section별 점수와 총점제공

*i*BT 시험 유형 세부 분석

*i*BT의 전체 시험 구성과 문항 수, 제한 시간은 다음과 같다.

Section	지문종류	지문	새로 추가된 종류
Reading		3~5 지문 (각 지문 당 12~14문제)	- 전문용어를 설명하는 Glossary - Multiple focus 정보를 분류하거나 summary를 완성 하는 문제 추가
Listening	Lecture	4~6 지문 (각 지문 당 6문제)	- Replay 문제 추가 - note-taking 허락
	Conversation	2~3 지문 (각 지문 당 5문제)	
Break	10분		
Speaking	Speaking	2문제	경험 또는 의견 말하기

	Reading →
	Listening
	→Speaking
		2문제	- 제시된 안건을 읽고 그 안건에 대한
			  강의를 듣고 정리해서 말하기
			- 제시된 안건을 읽고 안건에 대한 대화를
			  듣고 정리해서 말하기

	Listening →Speaking	2문제	- 강의를 듣고 요약하여 말하기 - 대화를 듣고 요약해서 말하기
Writing	Writing on topic	1개의 토픽	제시된 안건에 대한 의견 쓰기
	Reading → Listening → Writing	1개의 토픽	읽고 들은 내용에 근거하여 요점을 정리하여 논리적으로 쓰기

*i*BT Total Score Range Comparisons

Internet-Based Total	Computer-Based Total	Percentile Rank
111 - 120	273 - 300	97.6 - 100
96 - 110	243 - 270	85.9 - 96.8
79 - 95	213 - 240	64.8 - 85.0
65 - 78	183 - 210	45.6 - 63.6
53 - 64	153 - 180	29.9 - 44.3
41 - 52	123 - 150	16.7 - 28.6
30 - 40	93 - 120	7.4 - 15.8
19 - 29	63 - 90	1.7 - 6.5
9 - 18	33 - 60	0.1 - 1.2
0 - 8	0 - 30	0.04

*i*BT Reading Section의 구성

· **문제 유형으로 본 Reading Section에서 요하는 Reading Skills**

1. Basic Comprehension Questions

- 핵심 내용 또는 중요한 정보를 지문 내에서 빨리 효과적으로 찾아내는 능력
- 주제 또는 요지, 중요한 사실과 세부 내용, 문맥상의 어휘의 뜻, 지시어가 지칭하는 것이 무엇인지 파악하는 능력
- 복잡한 문법 구조를 가진 긴 문장의 해당 핵심 내용을 파악하는 능력

2. Inferencing Reading Questions

- 특정 소재를 언급한 작가의 의도, 특정 소재가 단락/지문 내에서 하는 역할, 작가의 주장을 전개해나가는 글의 구조를 파악할 줄 아는 능력
- 글의 논리적 전개에 따라 특정 문장을 올바르게 삽입하여 글의 유기적 통일성을 완성하는 능력
- 암시되어 있는 내용이 무엇인지 유추하는 능력

3. Reading to Learn Questions

- 지문의 전체적인 구조와 단락간의 관계를 인식하는 능력
- 지문 내에 표출되는 여러 내용 간의 관계를 이해하는 능력(접속사의 역할을 제대로 이해하는 것이 요)
- 주어진 여러 개의 정보를 올바르게 분류하는 능력
- 지문 내의 중요한 정보와 핵심적인 세부 사항을 기억하여 간략히 요약할 줄 아는 능력

· Reading section의 형식과 특징

지문 길이	지문 수와 문제 수	시간
600~700단어	3-5개 지문 지문 당 12~14개 문제	60 ~100분

1 각 지문마다 제목이 제시되기 때문에 main topic 고르는 문제는 출제되지 않는다. main idea 구하는 문제도 출제되지 않을 확률이 높음.

2 새로운 문제 유형이 생겨났다.

▶ **Prose Summary** : introductory sentence를 제시해주고, 지문을 잘 요약할 수 있는 문장 3개를 6개의 보기 안에서 드래그하여 완성하기(부분 점수 있음)

▶ **Schematic Table** : 지문에 제시되는 두 개의 대상에 대해 맞는 이야기를 하는 phrases를 올바르게 분류하여 차트 완성하기. 7개에서 5개 고르는 유형(2개는 지문에 언급되지 않는 내용)과 9개에서 7개 고르는 유형(2개는 지문에 언급되지 않는 내용)이 있음. 지문 전체의 구조와 세부 내용 간의 관계를 이해할 필요 있음.(부분 점수 있음)

▶ **Sentence Simplification** : 지문에 하이라이트된 문장의 핵심 정보를 가장 적절히 paraphrase한 문장 고르기. 처리해야하는 문장이 문법적으로 복잡한 구조를 가지고 있다는 것이 특징임.

▶ **Rhetorical Purpose** : 단어 또는 소개하는 내용이 갖는 수사학적인 목적을 파악하는 문제. 저자가 어떤 의도 및 목적으로 그 단어 또는 내용을 사용하는 지를 이해해야 함.

3 CBT에 없는 새로운 기능이 첨가되었다.

▶ **Glossary** : 지문에 파란색으로 밑줄 그어진 단어를 클릭하면 그 단어에 대한 영문 설명이 나오는 팝업창 뜸.

▶ **Review** : 문항에 대한 응답 상태를 확인할 수 있고, Go To Question 아이콘들을 이용하여 Review 화면에서 미응답 문제로 바로 이동 가능.

4 기타

▶ 문제 배점은 대부분 1점씩, Prose Summary와 Schematic Table 문제에는 2~4점이 주어짐.

▶ 한 지문 내에 Prose Summary 문제와 Schematic Table 문제가 동시에 출제되지 음.

MAIN IDEA

OVERVIEW

Main Idea 문제는 수업이나 대화에서 중점적으로 이야기하고자 하는 것, 즉 주제를 찾는 문제이다. 강의나 토론에서는 주로 다루어지고 있는 내용이 무엇인지를 찾고, 대화에서는 대화의 목적을 찾는다.

Question Types

What is the talk mainly about?
What is the topic of the talk?
What is the lecture mainly about?
Why does the man go to see the woman?
Why does the woman want to see the professor?
What does the student need from the counselor?

General Strategies

1 강의의 토픽 (Topic) 찾기

강의의 경우 시작부분이나 끝부분을 주목해서 듣는다. 이 때 화자의 signal을 통해 주제를 예측할 수 있다.

– 강의 도입 부분의 Signal

Today, I will tell you what ~ is about.
Today, we're going to talk about ~
I'd like to focus on ~ today.
Let's look for the aspects of ~ today.
What is your opinion about ~?

– 강의 마지막 부분의 Signal

Therefore ~, Thus[So] ~, In conclusion ~, For all of these reasons ~, These examples show ~

2 대화의 목적 (Purpose) 찾기

- 대화의 목적이란, 화자가 교수를 찾아온 이유가 무엇인지, 왜 상담원을 찾아갔는지, 도서관 직원으로부터 원하는 것이 무엇인지 등을 가리킨다. 화자는 처음부터 목적을 밝히기도 하지만 2~3차례 대화가 진행되면서 (A-B-A-B-A) 그 목적이 나타나기도 한다.

SAMPLE

TOEFL Listening

HIDE TIME 00:00:00

🎧 **Listen to a lecture in a biology class then answer the question.**

(P=W)

> **Professor**   Antibiotics play a major role in our society. Antibiotics stop living bacteria from multiplying or they kill them. Some antibiotics are produced naturally from living organisms such as fungi or molds. Others are wholly or in part synthetic – that is, produced artificially by scientists. Penicillin is perhaps the best known antibiotic that comes in both natural and artificial forms. Its discovery is among mankind's greatest achievements: it has saved millions of lives. Antibiotics have enabled the medical profession to treat many infectious diseases effectively making many no longer life-threatening.

What is the lecture mainly about?

(A) The value of antibiotics
(B) A special kind of medicine called penicillin
(C) The origins of antibiotics
(D) The side effects of antibiotics

해설

주제를 묻는 문제의 경우, 전반적인 내용을 전부 이해하기에 앞서 핵심 시그널이 될 부분을 파악해 두는 것이 중요하다. 강의 첫 부분에서 교수는 'Antibiotics play a major role in our society.'라고 언급함으로써 앞으로 항생물질의 중요성에 대해 살펴볼 것임을 암시했다.

Word Preview

☐ statement _____   ☐ research _____

🎧 **Listen to the following and answer the question.**

Why does the woman go to see the man?

(A) To get some advice on writing the essay

(B) To ask where to find information for the essay

ORGANIZATION   **Choose the best answer to complete the outline of the passage below.**

Woman's Problem
Essay: _____ ; not a question

↓

Solution
1. turn a statement into a _____
2. decide what to _____
3. get the answers

(a) research   (b) question   (c) a statement

DICTATION 🎧 **Listen again and fill in the blanks.**   (S1=W, S2=M)

Student 1   Can you help me?

Student 2   What's wrong?

Student 1   This essay, I have _____.

Student 2   _____, just answer the question!

Student 1   But look! It isn't a question.

Student 2   Hmmm…You're right, _____. Do you know _____ when they give me a statement not a question?

Student 1   No, what?

Student 2   I _____ a question by asking questions about everything in the statement and…

Student 1   Wait, _____! The questions that I ask tell me _____ _____!

Student 2   Yes! When you have questions you know what research _____ the answers.

Student 1   Whew! Thanks! Now I know how to _____ this essay.

✔ **Check-up** **for Vocabulary**

Choose the correct word in the box to complete the phrases.

turn it into	work on	statement	research

1   _____ the new project   3   _____ English

2   market _____   4   make a _____

Word Preview

☐ perception _____ ☐ beholder _____ ☐ equal _____
☐ concept _____

🎧 **Listen to the following and answer the question.**

What is the lecture mainly going to be about?

(A) What advertising does to our view of perfection in women

(B) What advertising does to our view of healthy women

ORGANIZATION Choose the best answer to complete the outline of the passage below.

Changes on perception of _____ caused by _____

In the past		In the present
– thin people equaled _____ people	→	– _____ is the ideal image of beauty

(a) advertising   (b) hungry and sick   (c) thiness   (d) the female perfection

20

DICTATION 🎧 **Listen again and fill in the blanks.**   (P=W)

Professor   Today I'd like to focus on _____ our perception of the female. One of these effects could be women's desire of being perfect size. This is because how women are portrayed in most ads. But beauty is most definitely _____ the beholder! In some centuries physically ideal women _____. We celebrate thinness _____ beauty, but in the past _____ unhealthiness: thin people _____ _____, sick people. Later, when you write your essays, I will expect you to demonstrate this concept; that beauty _____, but a media construct: in other words _____.

✔ **Check-up** **for Vocabulary**

Choose the correct word in the box to complete the phrases.

concept	celebrate	ideal	advertise	demonstrate	indicate

1 _____ Christmas

2 a(n) _____ world

3 _____ a house for sale

4 _____ a place on the street

5 _____ how to use the machine

6 a new _____ of the universe

Word Preview

☐ anorexia _____   ☐ anorexia nervosa _____   ☐ anorexia athletica _____
☐ bulimia _____   ☐ binge eating _____

Listen to the following and answer the question.

What is the talk mainly going to be about?

(A) Different types of eating disorders

(B) Different causes of eating disorders

ORGANIZATION   Choose the best answer to complete the outline of the passage below.

Eating Disorders

|

Types

• **Anorexia Nervosa**
: _____

• _____
: avoid food and lose too much weight

• **Bulimia**
: _____

• _____
: consuming extremely large amounts of food

|

Causes

Biological, _____, Social

(a) mental   (b) a fear of eating   (c) eating then vomiting   (d) binge eating   (e) anorexia athletica

DICTATION 🎧 **Listen again and fill in the blanks.**   (P=M, S=W)

Professor	Eating disorders _____. Let's begin with the following kinds; anorexia nervosa, anorexia athletica, bulimia, and binge eating. Can any of you define these conditions for me?
Student	Anorexia nervosa is _____; anorexia athletica is where athletes _____ and lose too much weight; bulimia is _____ to empty the stomach; and binge eating is consuming _____ food in a single meal.
Professor	Correct! Well done! People with these disorders can _____. So it is vital that we _____ and detect eating problems early, so that people can return to a normal life _____ possible. Today _____ _____ some of the major reasons for this happening. We will consider biological, mental, and social causes.

✔ **Check-up** for Vocabulary
....

Choose the correct word in the box to complete the phrases.

detect	warn	vital	consume	disorder	empty

1 _____ the trash   4 _____ of danger

2 _____ crimes   5 _____ gas

3 mental _____   6 a(n) _____ wound

Word Preview

☐ tribal _____ ☐ bush _____ ☐ civilization _____
☐ headdress _____ ☐ supernatural _____

🎧 **Listen to the following and answer the question.**

What is the lecture mainly about?

(A) The role of traditional African art

(B) The themes of traditional African art

ORGANIZATION **Choose the best answer to complete the outline of the passage below.**

African Traditional Art

1. First theme	2. Second theme	3. Third theme
_____ vs _____	Relationships between _____	Effort to _____ natural or supematural power

(a) Nature (b) control (c) sexes (d) Civilization

DICTATION 🎧 **Listen again and fill in the blanks.**   (P=M)

Professor   Traditional art _____ in the day to day life of African tribal society. Together _____ the three basic themes of African art. The first is the dualism between bush and village; nature verses civilization. _____ _____ or headdresses, African tribes express those ideas. The second is the relationships _____. African tribes _____ the problems and issues between man and woman relationships. The third theme is the _____ _____ natural or supernatural power. They often use masks _____ to please and honor the forces that affect _____.

✔ **Check-up** **for Vocabulary**

Choose the correct word in the box to complete the phrases.

deal with   traditional   explore   civilization   theme   relationship

1 _____ remote islands

2 Western _____

3 _____ the situation

4 a parent-child _____

5 the _____ of a music

6 _____ dress or food

 **Exercise 1**

TOEFL Listening

VOLUME ◀)))   HELP ?   OK ✓   NEXT ➜

HIDE TIME   00:00:00

🎧 **Listen to a discussion in a music class then answer the questions.**

1 What is the discussion mainly about?

(A) Punk rock's effect on government

(B) The changes in punk rock

(C) The negative effects of punk rock

(D) The commercialism of punk rock

2 According to the professor, what is original punk rock?

(A) Very emotional music that protests corrupt governments

(B) Entertaining music that makes people happy

(C) Powerful music that protests entertainment

(D) Emotional music that talks about the need for change

🎧 **Listen again and fill in the blanks. You may use your notes to help you answer the questions.**

Punk Rock   ┌ Original punk rock

         │   – feelings about _____ and _____

         └ Modern punk rock

            – more _____ / less _____

            – lyrics on _____ and _____

Exercise 2

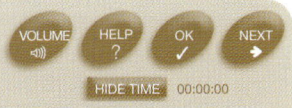

TOEFL Listening

VOLUME ◁)) HELP ? OK ✓ NEXT ➜

HIDE TIME 00:00:00

🎧 **Listen to a talk in a medical class then answer the questions.**

1 What is the talk mainly about?

(A) The importance of good Qi

(B) What Americans prefer

(C) How acupuncture works

(D) Why drugs are no good

2 According to the professor, why do Americans think acupuncture is better than modern drugs?

(A) Acupuncture reduces symptoms.

(B) Acupuncture increases health.

(C) Acupuncture works faster.

(D) Acupuncture cures the causes.

🎧 **Listen again and fill in the blanks. You may use your notes to help you answer the questions.**

Acupuncture

    (1) being healed _____ into specific points of the body

    (2) restores balance between _____

    (3) _____

 **Exercise 3**

TOEFL Listening

VOLUME HELP ? OK ✓ NEXT →

HIDE TIME 00:00:00

🎧 **Listen to a lecture in a business class then answer the questions.**

1 **What is the lecture mainly about?**

(A) How to start a business

(B) How to avoid failure and be successful

(C) The importance of having a business plan

(D) The importance of operating budget

2 **According to the professor, which of the following is NOT a key factor?**

(A) Finding out if people need the product

(B) Creating an operating budget

(C) Estimating time before profit

(D) Providing good products

🎧 **Listen again and fill in the blanks. You may use your notes to help you answer the questions.**

Three Keys of _____

   1. Determining if _____

   2. Establishing _____

   3. Estimating how long it will take to _____

Exercise 4

TOEFL Listening

🎧 **Listen to a conversation between a student and a counselor then answer the questions.**

1 **Why does the man go to the woman?**
   (A) To ask if he can find another roommate
   (B) To find a single dorm
   (C) To get off campus list
   (D) To get a job off campus

2 **What was the man's problem?**
   (A) He couldn't sleep well.
   (B) He couldn't find a classmate.
   (C) He couldn't change rooms.
   (D) He couldn't do his work.

🎧 **Listen again and fill in the blanks. You may use your notes to help you answer the questions.**

Problem : The man _____

     → because of _____

Option : 1. _____

     2. _____

     3. _____

Dictation for Exercise

Exercise 1

🎧 **Listen and fill in the blanks.**   (P=M, S1=W, S2=M)

Professor	Punk rock ① _____ express feelings about corrupt governments and other ② _____. Modern punk rock ③ _____ more about entertainment and less about protest.
Student 1	Well... ④ _____ because modern punk rock lyrics are more about relationships and life and sometimes the songs and groups are now ⑤ _____. It's like we have two forms of punk rock; modern and primitive.
Student 2	I don't agree. I think that modern punk rock ⑥ _____ _____, it's something different: ⑦ _____. Groups became commerical. They became money focused!
Professor	Well, yes, some people have suggested that they sold out, however, ⑧ _____ to survive? I'd suggest that it had to become more commercial to find ⑨ _____.

|구문해설| **corrupt government** 부패한 정부   **social issue** 사회적 문제   **make sense** 이치에 닿다, 뜻이 통하다   **lyric** 서정시, 가사   **primitive** 원시의, 초기의   **no longer** 더 이상 ~ 아니다   **sell out** 배반하다; 팔다

✔ Check-up for Expression

Complete the sentences using given words or phrases.

make sense	social issue	be created to

1 Do you believe his opinion _____?

2 A special committee _____ deal with the problem.

3 The purpose of the meeting is to discuss _____ such as education, environmental pollution.

Exercise 2

🎧 **Listen and fill in the blanks.**   (P=M, S=W)

Professor	Many Americans ① _____ acupuncture to deal with health issues. Acupuncture can be defined ② _____ inserting needles into specific points of the body.
Student	Why do they think that's better than modern drugs?
Professor	Good question! The idea is drugs only ③ _____ but acupucture ④ _____.
Student	How?
Professor	Well, this is the idea that we need ⑤ _____ 'Qi' to be healthy. 'Qi' is believed to be the basic energy that constitutes everything that exists. In our bodies there are two opposing forces, 'yin'(water), and 'yang'(fire). ⑥ _____ this blocks the flow of 'Qi' through our bodies ⑦ _____. Sticking needles in specific parts of the body ⑧ _____, 'Qi' flows again, and good health is restored.

|구문해설| **acupuncture** 침술   **insert ~ into...** ~을 ...에 삽입하다   **symptom** 증상; 징후, 징조   **unobstructed** 방해받지 않은
constitute 구성하다, 구성 요소가 되다   **out of balance** 평형을 잃고, 불안정하여   **opposing** 반대하는, 반하는
restore balance 균형을 되찾다

✔ **Check-up** for Expression
┈┈

Complete the sentences using given words or phrases.

turn to	be defined as	out of balance

1 Reports warn the tax system is _____.

2 Democracy _____ "rule by the people."

3 He has no one to _____ here because he immigrated from China just a month ago.

Exercise 3

🎧 **Listen and fill in the blanks.** (P=M)

Professor   Today we will look at planning. There is a saying ① '_____

_____!' Yes, I can see ② _____ that nobody plans

to fail. However, many businesses do fail because they don't plan. In a

business plan there are three key factors: determining ③ _____

_____, establishing an operating budget, and estimating ④ _____

_____ to make a profit. Many great products have failed because there

was no market need. It does not matter that a product is great. ⑤ _____

_____ enough people want to buy that product. Many companies

go bankrupt because they ⑥ _____ and overspend. It is also

⑦ _____ money into a business hoping it will

eventually become successful. We have to know when to give up. Planning

⑧ _____ success but failing to plan can guarantee failure.

|구문해설| **key factor** 주요 요소   **operating budget** 업무 예산   **make a profit** 이윤을 내다   **what matters is** ~ 중요한 것은
~이다   **go bankrupt** 파산하다   **overspend** 낭비하다

✔ **Check-up** for Expression

Complete the sentences using given words or phrases.

make a profit	go bankrupt	give up

1 If we can't _____ with this new product, we will go out of business.

2 Once you made up your mind, do not _____ halfway.

3 Because of a long economic slump, many corporations may _____ in the
near future.

Exercise 4

🎧 **Listen and fill in the blanks.**

(S=M, C=W)

Student   Excuse me! Can you help me?

Counselor ① _____! What do you need?

Student   I'm not happy ② _____, I want to move.

Counselor Oh! I'm sorry to hear that. What's the problem?

Student   I can't study because ③ _____. I'd like to know if there is ④ _____.

Counselor Well, let's see! Hmmm… just as I thought, ⑤ _____.

Student   Well, what can I do? ⑥ _____ I have to keep living with this guy.

Counselor You could try a different roommate. I have a list here of students looking for someone to share their dorm. Or you ⑦ _____ off campus accommodation list.

Student   Okay, can I have ⑧ _____? I'll try them both.

Counselor Sure, you can have these. Good luck!

|구문해설| **dorm** 기숙사(= dormitory)   **available** 사용[이용]할 수 있는   **accommodation** 숙박 설비

✔ Check-up for Expression

Complete the sentences using given words or phrases.

off campus	available	go mad

1 Is the meeting room _____ tomorrow evening?

2 He _____ when the computer went down again.

3 Most of the students live _____, not in dorms.

Vocabulary Review

Write the meanings of the words or phrases in the blanks.

1	theme	_____	21	accommodation	_____
2	perception	_____	22	thin	_____
3	consume	_____	23	vomit	_____
4	vital	_____	24	empty	_____
5	detect	_____	25	warn	_____
6	beholder	_____	26	disorder	_____
7	anorexia	_____	27	unobstructed	_____
8	antibiotic	_____	28	opposing	_____
9	bulimia	_____	29	overspend	_____
10	binge eating	_____	30	civilization	_____
11	tribal	_____	31	demonstrate	_____
12	infectious	_____	32	mental	_____
13	supernatural	_____	33	make a profit	_____
14	constitute	_____	34	out of balance	_____
15	available	_____	35	make sense	_____
16	lyric	_____	36	no longer	_____
17	primitive	_____	37	sell out	_____
18	acupuncture	_____	38	insert ~ into...	_____
19	symptom	_____	39	go bankrupt	_____
20	dorm	_____	40	deal with	_____

Chapter 02

SUPPORTING DETAILS

OVERVIEW

Detail 문제는 강의나 대화에서 화자가 말하고자 하는 것을 뒷받침하기 위해 언급한 구체적인 내용을 찾는 문제이다. 화자가 '직접 언급한 사실'을 토대로 답을 찾아야 하므로 짐작되거나 개인적인 추론을 바탕으로 답해서는 안 된다.

Question Types

What is the best definition for ~?
What does the professor say about ~?
What does the man want to know?
What is the man's suggestion for ~?
What evidence was given by the professor?
What is (NOT) true about ~?
Which of the following is the effect / feature / reason of ~?
According to the professor, what is ~?
According to the conversation, what is the man's problem?

General Strategies

1 강의의 Supporting Details 찾기

강의에서는 세세한 부분보다는 강의의 요점과 관련된 중요 핵심 정보를 물어 본다. 정의(definition) 예(example), 이유(reason), 결과(result), 문제점과 해결책(problem & solution), 특징(feature) 등이 이런 핵심 정보에 속한다. 중요하다고 생각되는 정보는 Note-taking하여 문제 풀이 시 참고하는 것이 좋다.

2 대화의 Supporting Details 찾기

대화는 A라는 화자가 지닌 문제점이나 그가 원하는 것에 대해 B라는 화자가 해결책을 제시하거나 조언해주는 내용으로 이루어져 있다. 그러므로 A라는 화자가 제시하는 문제점 혹은 그가 원하는 것이 무엇인지, 이에 대한 B의 반응이 어떤지 주의해서 들어야 한다.

TOEFL Listening

VOLUME 🔊 | HELP ? | OK ✓ | NEXT →

HIDE TIME 00:00:00

🎧 **Listen to a lecture in a biology class then answer the question.**

(P=M)

Professor In this lecture we are going to focus on the armadillo, one of nature's most unique creatures. What feature makes this animal so unique? A coat of armor! I can see some of you smiling now, but it's true, their bodies are covered with plates of bone. In addition to their armor, they have powerful claws. Some of you might think now that they are formidable animals, predators to avoid, but in fact they have no fighting instinct. They are burrowing animals that avoid conflict by digging holes. That's what the claws are for, to help them dig quickly. Of course they are not unique for their claws, or their lack of fighting instinct. Their coat of armor is their claim to fame: we might call them "nature's tanks."

According to the lecture, which of the following is NOT the feature of the armadillo?

(A) They live in a hole in the ground.

(B) They have very well protected bodies.

(C) They are very good at digging holes.

(D) They attack animals with their sharp claws.

해설

강의의 세부 사항을 묻는 문제의 경우, 답안지를 하나씩 확인하면서 정답과 오답을 체크해두는 것이 좋다. 아르마딜로의 특징은 크게 '갑옷 같은 몸체, 강력한 발톱, 굴 파기'로 들 수 있다. 특히 발톱은 구멍을 파는 데 쓰이는 것이다. 이들은 선투 본능이 없다고 했으므로 (D)는 답이 되지 않는다.

Word Preview

☐ switch _____

 **Listen to the following and answer the question.**

What is the reason the professor switched classrooms?

(A) Because he needs more space for his class.

(B) Because his room is under repair.

ORGANIZATION Choose the best answer to complete the outline of the passage below.

Woman's problem	Professor's problem
↓	↓
Cause · was _____ · didn't see _____ on the door	**Solution** · switched classrooms from _____ to _____

(a) Room 801　(b) Room 806　(c) a notice　(d) late for class

DICTATION 🎧 Listen again and fill in the blanks. (S=W, P=M)

Student	Excuse me! Sorry I'm late everyone… Oh! Do we have a new professor?
Professor	No, I think you _____.
Student	But _____?
Professor	Yes, this is Room 801 but _____ a different classroom. Your professor and I _____ _____ because I _____. There is a notice on the door if you look.
Student	Oh! I'm so sorry, Professor. _____ I didn't see it.
Professor	You need to go to Room 806, _____. Next time, please make sure you look before you enter a room. Besides, you shouldn't be late anyway. Now, where was I?
Student	Yes sir, sorry, bye.

✔ Check-up for Vocabulary

Choose the correct word in the box to complete the phrases.

switch	space	enter	notice

1 official _____

2 parking _____

3 ___ ___ the house

4 _____ seats

Skill Check-up 2

Word Preview

☐ speck _____   ☐ particulate _____   ☐ hydrocarbon _____
☐ lead _____

🎧 Listen to the following and answer the question.

According to the professor, what are particulates?

(A) Tiny bits of dust angels that make ozone

(B) Tiny bits of products left in the air after burning wood, coal, and oil

ORGANIZATION

Choose the best answer to complete the outline of the passage below.

Particulates = _____

↓

burn _____ , oil

↓

leave _____ in the air

↓

We breathe in _____

(a) wood, coal   (b) small solid particules   (c) unburned products   (d) the remains

DICTATION 🎧 **Listen again and fill in the blanks.**   (P=M, S=W)

Professor	You might think _____ the effects of pollution in this room, but are we really? Can you see the tiny specks _____? They look beautfiul, don't they? But they can also be deadly. What is it that _____?
Student	Well, isn't it just harmless dust? I remember that my grandmother _____ 'dust angels.'
Professor	Well, we call them particulates. What you are really seeing are small solid particles _____ from the things we _____ our civilization, such as wood, coal, and oil. We _____ the remains of our civilization everyday: unburned hydrocarbons, ozone and lead.
Student	Now I understand why you say _____.

✔ Check-up for Vocabulary

Choose the correct word in the box to complete the phrases.

deadly	harmless	pollution	safe	burn	solid

1 a(n) _____ poison

2 environmental _____

3 _____ wood

4 _____ insects

5 feel _____

6 _____ shell

Word Preview

☐ twinkle _____ ☐ atmosphere _____ ☐ horizon _____

🎧 **Listen to the following and answer the question.**

According to the lecture, what is the reason stars twinkle?

(A) Because starlight is bent by the Earth's atmosphere.

(B) Because stars move in the Earth's atmosphere.

ORGANIZATION **Choose the best answer to complete the outline of the passage below.**

Why stars _____

↓

1. their light _____ atmosphere

↓

2. their light travels through the _____

↓

3. it _____ many times in all directions

(a) passes through   (b) layers of atmosphere   (c) is bent   (d) twinkle

DICTATION 🎧 Listen again and fill in the blanks. (P=W)

Professor Why do stars twinkle? Well, the reason's because their light _____ our atmosphere before _____ _____. As their light travels through the many layers of the Earth's atmosphere, _____ in various directions, so it looks like the star is moving. _____ _____ everyone would see that there are no twinkling stars. They don't move. Tonight, when we look at stars I want _____ an experiment. Look at the stars overhead and then at the stars _____. You should see that the stars closer to the horizon will seem to twinkle more than _____. That's because _____ has to travel _____ to reach you.

✔ Check-up for Vocabulary

Choose the correct word in the box to complete the phrases.

direction	outer	twinkle	bend	experiment	pass through

1 _____ suburbs

2 _____ the body

3 _____ a tunnel

4 a chemical _____

5 _____ brightly

6 in every _____

Word Preview

☐ progressive _____ ☐ depression _____ ☐ urine _____

🎧 **Listen to the following and answer the question.**

According to the lecture, what can be a symptom of Huntington's disease?

(A) Problem walking

(B) Problem urinating

ORGANIZATION Choose the best answer to complete the outline of the passage below.

Huntington's Disease

Cause

: _____

Symptom

· mental

: _____

· physical

: _____

Diagnosis

: _____

(a) a single gene   (b) depression   (c) urine analysis   (d) an unsteady walk

Lecture

DICTATION 🎧 Listen again and fill in the blanks. (P=W)

Professor   As doctors you will have to diagnose or identify _____ _____ diseases. Huntington's disease _____ _____. This is a progressive, neurological disease _____ _____. What are the symptoms to look for? It depends on the patient. _____ start with mental symptoms such as depression. Other patients _____ _____ such as _____. I'm not surprised you look worried; with symptoms like this it is very _____. So, _____, get a test done before you move on to other possible answers. OK! Now, let's move on to urine analysis and the role it can play in the early diagnosis of this disease.

* neurological 신경의, 신경학상의

✔ Check-up for Vocabulary

Choose the correct word in the box to complete the phrases.

depression	diagnose	unsteady	progressive	analysis	depend on

1 _____ development

2 suffer from _____

3 a critical _____

4 _____ cancer

5 _____ the weather

6 a(n) _____ idea

TOEFL Listening

VOLUME
◁))

HELP
?

OK
✓

NEXT
→

HIDE TIME 00:00:00

🎧 **Listen to a lecture in an art class then answer the questions.**

1 According to the lecture, what are two key methods the painter used in *The Persistence of Memory*? Choose TWO answers.

(A) Making things look like they are very unreal

(B) Making things look like they are a photograph

(C) Using weak shadows and lighter areas

(D) Using strong shadows and lighter areas

2 According to the professor, what do the four melted clocks symbolize?

(A) That we cannot really trust what we see.

(B) That we cannot really know the time.

(C) That time is something that keeps moving.

(D) That time is something that is hard to paint.

* chiaroscuro [미술] 명암법   * trompe l'oeil [미술] 실물처럼 보이는 그림

🎧 **Listen again and fill in the blanks. You may use your notes to help you answer the questions.**

Persistence of Memory – · Painted by ⬚

· Painted in ⬚

· Two effects – Contrast between ⬚

  – Photographic reality

· Represent – time is not ⬚

  time involves ⬚

 **Exercise 2**

TOEFL Listening

VOLUME 🔊 HELP ? OK ✓ NEXT →

HIDE TIME 00:00:00

🎧 **Listen to a talk in a fashion design class then answer the questions.**

1 **According to the professor, what is fashion in the 80s and 90s like?**

(A) Re-inventing fashions greatly changed

(B) Re-inventing past foreign fashions

(C) Re-inventing lots of foreign fashions in new ways

(D) Re-inventing old fashions using foreign ones

2 **According to the talk, which of the following is NOT true?**

(A) There are four very important periods of fashion.

(B) Since the 80s there have been no new fashion ideas.

(C) Revolution is the main concept of 1950s' fashion.

(D) In the 1940s they liked to wear hats.

* **shirtwaist** 셔츠웨이스트드레스(와이셔츠 모양으로 앞이 트인 원피스) * **afroes** 아프로 머리(흑인의 헤어스타일)

🎧 **Listen again and fill in the blanks. You may use your notes to help you answer the questions.**

Fashion's Evolution

	Feature		Details
1. 40s		→	elegant long dresses, hats
2. 50s		→	in the movie *Grease*
3. 60s		→	hippies; anti-tradition
4. 70s	Fun	→	platform shoes, afroes, bell-bottoms
⇒ 80/90s			

■Exercise 3

Discussion

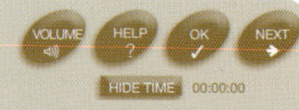

VOLUME HELP OK NEXT
? ✓ →

HIDE TIME 00:00:00

🎧 **Listen to a discussion in a business class then answer the questions.**

1 **According to the professor, what is e-business?**

(A) Buying and selling of goods using the Internet

(B) A system providing companies faster and easier Internet functions

(C) Trading goods in physical stores instead of using the Internet

(D) Traditional business between customers and buyers

2 **According to the discussion, which of the following is NOT the benefit of e-business?**

(A) People can buy things at home without going out.

(B) People can buy things at a lower price.

(C) People can track their order instantly.

(D) People can easily compare the product quality.

🎧 **Listen again and fill in the blanks. You may use your notes to help you answer the questions.**

E-business

Definition : _____ using the Internet

Benefits : 1. Do not need to _____

2. Compare _____

3. Buy goods at _____

Exercise 4

TOEFL Listening

VOLUME ◁◁)) HELP ? OK ✓ NEXT →

HIDE TIME 00:00:00

🎧 **Listen to a conversation between a student and a counselor then answer the questions.**

1 Which of the following is NOT the options the woman gives?

(A) Library worker

(B) Teaching assistant

(C) Student tutor

(D) Lab assistant

2 According to the woman, how can the man apply for the work he wants?

(A) Fill out an application form.

(B) Write a letter for an interview.

(C) Have an interview at the library.

(D) Write a letter to the woman.

🎧 **Listen again and fill in the blanks. You may use your notes to help you answer the questions.**

What the mans wants :

⇒ Three options : (1)

(2)

(3)

How to apply

:   →

Dictation for Exercise

Exercise 1

🎧 **Listen and fill in the blanks.**

(P=W)

Professor ① _____ you now is *The Persistence of Memory*: perhaps one of Salvador Dali's best known works. ② _____ Dali uses ③ _____ the effect that he wanted. For example, we have chiaroscuro. It is the use of light and shade in a picture; ④ _____. Another is trompe l'oeil. With this he tried to make people think that the objects are real. It is a style of painting that gives the illusion of photographic reality. Look now at the four melted clocks. They represent that time ⑤ _____ or fixed. ⑥ _____ reminding us that time flies; and the ants on another stating the fact that time involves decay. ⑦ _____ _____; how persistent is memory really? Let's discuss that now.

|구문해설| **portray** 그리다, 묘사하다 　**raise a question** 문제를 제기하다

✔ **Check-up** for Expression

Complete the sentences using given words or phrases.

try to	state	a style of

1 Please _____ finish this work by the end of this month.

2 When you write, it's important to develop _____ your own.

3 Do not _____ your own view unless he asks you first.

Exercise 2

🎧 **Listen and fill in the blanks.** (P=W, S1=M, S2=W)

Student1   What are the most ① _____ fashion, Professor?

Professor   I see ② _____ fashion's evolution: the 40s, feminine glamor, elegant long dresses, hats; the 50s, shirtwaist, perfectly represented in the movie *Grease* which ③ _____; the 60s, revolution, the anti-tradition movement of the hippies; and the 70s, fun, lots of platform shoes, afroes and bell-bottoms.

Student2   But what about the 80s and 90s? Don't we see lots of fashion there?

Professor   Yes, we see lots of fashion but ④ _____ existing fashions and re-inventing fashions of the past ⑤ _____ foreign fashions.

Student2   So, you're suggesting that we ⑥ _____ and since the 80s have simply ⑦ _____?

Professor   Yes, correct.

|구문해설| **feminine glamor** 여성적 매력   **anti-tradition movement** 반전통 운동, 전통에 반대하는 움직임   **platform shoes** 통굽 구두   **bell-bottoms** 나팔식 바지   **combine with ~** ~와 결합하다   **run out of ~** ~이 바닥나다, ~을 다 써버리다

✔ **Check-up** for Expression

Complete the sentences using given words or phrases.

combine with	run out of	an extension of

1   We couldn't move a mile. We _____ gas.

2   Hydrogen _____ oxygen to form water.

3   I'd like to get an answer on _____ the deadline.

Exercise 3

🎧 **Listen and fill in the blanks.**   (P=M, S1=W, S2=M)

Professor	Basically e-business means ① _____ using the Internet. Today there are millions of e-businesses on-line. Why do people buy things on-line ② _____?
Student 1	Well, ③ _____ convenience. The users do not need to go out shopping to buy things. They can make their purchase ④ _____ _____ where they can ⑤ _____ without going out.
Student 2	That's right. By using the Internet, not only will it make purchasing ⑥ _____, but they can also tell where to get the best quality and cheapest price by just clicking on the computer.
Professor	Great. OK. Then, ⑦ _____ be successful in e-business? Let's talk about it now.

|구문해설| **instead of ~** ~ 대신에   **a matter of ~** ~에 관한 문제   **get connected** (컴퓨터에) 연결되다   **without ~ing** ~하지 않고, ~ 없이

✔ **Check-up** for Expression
....

Complete the sentences using given words or phrases.

instead of	a matter of	get connected

1 You'd better consider the possibility of taking the train _____ an air plane.

2 I do not mean that it's difficult. It's just _____ interest.

3 If you want to get that information you should _____ to the Internet first.

Exercise 4

🎧 **Listen and fill in the blanks.**

(C=W, S=M)

Counselor   Hello! What can I do for you today?

Student   ① _____ you could help me find some part-time work.

Counselor   Yes, I can help you with that. What kind of work ② _____?

Student   I don't really want to work as a waiter or bar tender, ③ _____ office work.

Counselor   Well, we have several options we can look at ④ _____. The university library is looking for counter staff. I know that ⑤ _____ need assistants this year and ⑥ _____ student-tutors.

Student   Wow! All of those sound really interesting. The work in the library would be great. How do I apply?

Counselor   ⑦ _____ for me and ⑧ _____ for you.

Student   Thanks!

|구문해설| **office work** 사무, 사무 일   **help (a person) with ~** ~으로 남을 돕다   **arrange** 마련하다, 준비하다

✔ Check-up for Expression

Complete the sentences using given words or phrases.

arrange	fill in	help with

1   If you want to participate in the game, please _____ the form first.

2   You should _____ a meeting with the marketing team to discuss that matter.

3   Our committees are created to _____ problems that students are experiencing.

Vocabulary Review

Write the meanings of the words or phrases in the blanks.

1	era	_____	21	analysis	_____
2	space	_____	22	horizon	_____
3	enter	_____	23	progressive	_____
4	notice	_____	24	neurological	_____
5	speck	_____	25	depression	_____
6	particulate	_____	26	urine	_____
7	symptom	_____	27	portray	_____
8	lead	_____	28	diagnose	_____
9	gene	_____	29	unsteady	_____
10	elegant	_____	30	arrange	_____
11	switch	_____	31	atmosphere	_____
12	reinvention	_____	32	pass through ~	_____
13	application	_____	33	raise a question	_____
14	deadly	_____	34	combine with ~	_____
15	pollution	_____	35	run out of ~	_____
16	burn	_____	36	instead of ~	_____
17	harmless	_____	37	depend on ~	_____
18	safe	_____	38	a matter of ~	_____
19	twinkle	_____	39	get connected	_____
20	direction	_____	40	without ~ing	_____

PROCESS / CLASSIFICATION

OVERVIEW

Process 문제는 강의나 대화에서 드러나는 단계, 절차, 시간 상의 순서를, Classification 문제는 전체 내용을 어떤 기준에 따라 분류하여, 그 기준에 해당하는 것이 무엇인지를 묻는 문제이다.

Question Types

Which of the following are the steps of ~?
In what order does the professor talk about ~?
Indicate whether each of the following is a step in the process.
Which of the following can be an example of ~?
Classify the phrases below. Click on the correct box for each phrase.
What's the difference between ~?
According to the conversation, how does A differ from B?

General Strategies

1 단계 · 절차 (Process) 파악하기

대화나 강의에 언급된 정보를 특정 순서나 절차, 또는 연대순으로 정리하고 세부 사항을 메모한다. 화자는 자신이 언급할 내용을 한꺼번에 얘기한 다음 하나씩 풀어서 설명하는 경우도 있고, 한 가지 절차나 순서를 언급하고 그것에 관해 구체적인 것을 설명하는 방식으로 넘어가는 경우도 있다. 순서나 절차의 이름은 어려운 단어로 되어 있는 경우가 많으므로, 그에 따르는 설명을 잘 듣도록 한다.

2 내용 분류하기 (Classification)

대화나 강의에서 화자가 무엇을 분류하는지, 분류된 대상은 무엇인지, 그리고 분류된 대상에 대한 각각의 설명은 어떤 것인지를 메모한다. 분류된 대상을 두고 비교 혹은 대조하는 경우도 있으므로 두 대상 사이에 어떤 유사점과 차이점이 있는지도 주목해야 한다.

SAMPLE

🎧 **Listen to a lecture in a biology class then answer the question.**

(P=W)

Professor Throughout this series of lectures we have discussed the question 'Are humans animals?' Today we are going to focus on the differences that exist between humans and apes. We will examine the following elements: movement, physical structure, etc. Alright, concerning movement, humans are bipedal, in other words we walk in an upright position. Primates might sometimes walk upright but normally, as you know, they use their arms and legs to walk. Physical structure is also different. Humans have a unique 'S' shaped spine; primates a round, arched spine. Another unique feature is the fact that human hands are shorter and broader, containing more muscle attachments. As a result they are stronger and more precise than that of primates or any other animal.

In the lecture, the professor describes the differences between humans and apes. Indicate the correct description for each item.

	Humans	Apes
They walk in an upright position.		
They have round arched spine.		
They usually move on all fours.		
Their hands contain more muscle attachments.		

해설

인간 – 직립 자세 / S형 척추 / 짧고 넓은 손, 더 많은 근육으로 정밀한 움직임을 보인다.
영장류 – 네발로 걷기 / 둥근 아치형 척추 / 손의 경우, 인간과 영장류를 비교한 점으로 짐작 가능하다.

Word Preview

☐ encode _____ ☐ retain _____ ☐ retrieve _____

🎧 **Listen to the following and answer the question.**

Check the correct box to indicate whether each of the following is a step in the process.

	Yes	No
Like a computer we hold information by turning it into a code.		
We retain the information like a computer memory.		
We store information in our short-term memory.		
We retrieve information as needed.		

ORGANIZATION

Choose the best answer to complete the outline of the passage below.

Memory : Information Process

_____ → _____ → Get back when needed by _____

· Store in _____
· _____ – rapidly lost

(a) short-term memory   (b) long-term memory   (c) retain   (d) encode   (e) retrieving

DICTATION 🎧 **Listen again and fill in the blanks.** (P=W)

Professor   Memory is an information process, somewhat similar to a computer information-processing system: _____ _____. First we use _____; which is getting information into our brain, to obtain information. And then we retain that information like a computer memory. We _____ information in our long-term memory. Finally we get the information back _____ by retrieving information. However, humans also possess short-term memory. This is activated memory holding information _____, such as phone numbers needed when dialing. If such information does not pass to the long-term memory _____.

✔ **Check-up** for Vocabulary

Choose the correct word in the box to complete the phrases.

encode	obtain	store	long-term	a great deal of	brief

1 a(n) _____ note   4 _____ great fame

2 _____ data   5 _____ food for the winter

3 take _____ time   6 a(n) _____ contract

Word Preview

☐ explosion _____ ☐ dominant _____

🎧 **Listen to the following and answer the question.**

Indicate the correct statement for each theory.

	Big Bang	Steady State
The universe has never changed.		
The universe came from this event.		
Scientists prefer this theory now.		
The universe is eternal.		

ORGANIZATION — **Choose the best answer to complete the outline of the passage below.**

The Origins of the Universe

Big Bang
- · _____
- · _____
- · _____

Steady State
- · _____
- · always been the same
- · less accepted

(a) a huge explosion (b) changing (c) dominant theory (d) no beginning

DICTATION 🎧 **Listen again and fill in the blanks.** (P=M, S=W)

Professor There have been two major theories for _____ _____; Big Bang and Steady State. The Big Bang theory suggests the universe had a beginning, _____ a huge explosion. The Steady State theory _____ _____ the universe did not begin, _____ _____. Also, the Big Bang universe is a place that's significantly different today _____. As we move outwards from the center of the universe _____ _____ quasars that appear to have _____ existence. _____ in the Steady State universe things have _____ and therefore there's nothing new.

Student So... which theory is more accepted?

Professor For many years Steady State was the leading theory but now Big Bang is dominant.

* quasar 준성, 항성상

✔ **Check-up** **for Vocabulary**
. . . .

Choose the correct word in the box to complete the phrases.

| origin | huge | outwards | item | leading | dominant |

1 a news _____

2 a(n) _____ ship

3 travel _____ into space

4 the _____ party

5 a(n) _____ businessman

6 the _____ of the civilization

Word Preview

☐ consist _____   ☐ opponent _____

🎧 **Listen to the following and answer the question.**

Indicate the correct statement for each tribe.

	Cherokee	Iroquois
It was a great game for war.		
Players used sticks to injure their opponents.		
It was very well organized.		
The goals were only 120 feet apart.		

ORGANIZATION   **Choose the best answer to complete the outline of the passage below.**

The Origins of Lacrosse

Cherokee

· _____
· hundreds/thousands
· _____
· _____

········· Purpose ·········
········· Players ·········
········· Goals ·········
········· Focus ·········

Iroquois

· _____
· maximum 15
· 120 feet apart
· _____

(a) military training   (b) miles apart   (c) hitting the ball   (d) hitting the players   (e) game only

DICTATION 🎧 **Listen again and fill in the blanks.**　　　　(P=W)

Professor　So everyone, just where did lacrosse come from? Well, _____, it was invented by Native Americans. Two of the main Indian tribes that _____ this sport were... the Cherokee and the Iroquois. The Cherokees used it _____ military training but for the Iroquois it was _____. The former had teams _____ _____ hundreds, sometimes thousands of players. The goals were miles apart and games _____ or even days. Players focused more on _____ with their sticks than _____. By comparison the Iroquois had a very organized and more sports orientated game. Teams consisted of only 12 to 15 players each and the goals were only about 120 _____.

* **Cherokee** 체로키 족 (Oklahoma 주에 많이 사는 북미 인디언)
* **Iroquois** 이로쿼이 족 (New York 주에 살았던 아메리칸 인디언)

✔ **Check-up** for Vocabulary

Choose the correct word in the box to complete the phrases.

tribe	participate in	training	last	injure	organized

1 an African _____
2 _____ for 3 hours
3 _____ your health
4 _____ management
5 a well _____ group
6 professional _____

Word Preview

□ try out _____ □ medical _____ □ fit _____

🎧 **Listen to the following and answer the question.**

Choose the correct and incorrect statements for each box.

To be on the team	Yes	No
You must be very healthy.		
You have to play with the team first.		
You have to show how well you can play the game.		
You must join the workout club.		
You have to pass a written test.		

ORGANIZATION — **Choose the best answer to complete the outline of the passage below.**

Man
- wants to _____
- needs to _____, train with team
  → the coach will _____ if he is good enough
- will _____

(a) watch and decide (b) take a medical (c) join a school activity club (d) join workout club

DICTATION 🎧 **Listen again and fill in the blanks.**   (S1=M, S2=W)

Student 1   I want to join a school activity club, maybe football or baseball.

Student 2   Well, if you want to do that then you _____. You can't just join those clubs. You _____ you are good enough _____.

Student 1   How do I do that?

Student 2   First you _____; then you join Saturday training _____.

Student 1   Join training with the team?

Student 2   Yes, it's for the coach. You have to play in a practice game and the coach _____ if you are good enough.

Student 1   So I _____?

Student 2   Yes, boys have to be very _____. Why not join my workout club first and _____?

Student 1   But I thought your club was _____.

Student 2   Oh no! Boys can join, too!

✔ **Check-up** for Vocabulary

Choose the correct word in the box to complete the phrases.

join	prove	medical	workout

1   _____ a club

2   _____ the innocence

3   a total-body _____

4   have a(n) _____ check-up

 **Exercise 1**

Talk in a Class

TOEFL Listening

VOLUME HELP ? OK ✓ NEXT →

HIDE TIME 00:00:00

🎧 **Listen to a talk in a politics class then answer the questions.**

1 Check the correct box to indicate which statement is true.

	Yes	No
Party members elects a candidate that will represent their party.		
Presidential electors vote for who will be President.		
The people in each state directly select President.		
The electoral College is a method by which presidents are chosen.		

2 According to the professor, what is the Electoral College?

(A) A method of learning how to vote

(B) The popular candinates in each state

(C) The best way to elect a president

(D) Electors who cast their votes for presidential candinate

🎧 **Listen again and fill in the blanks. You may use your notes to help you answer the questions.**

The Process of _____

1. Party members   : _____ who represents their party
2. Voters in each state : cast their vote for _____
3. _____   : as many electors as each state's representatives and senators
                          : cast their votes for their state's preferred candidate
4. Winning candidate   : _____ , become president

66

Exercise 2

TOEFL Listening

VOLUME HELP OK NEXT

HIDE TIME 00:00:00

🎧 **Listen to a conversation between a professor and a student then answer the questions.**

1 Identify the following and click on the correct box for each statement.

	Poem	Essay
You should write it in blank verse.		
You should review academic literature about grace.		
You should use less than 300 words.		
You must show where the work came from.		

2 What does the professor say about the deadline?

(A) Hand in when you finish.

(B) You have two weeks to finish.

(C) You must finish it before the end of the month.

(D) You can hand in after the last lesson.

* blank verse 무운시

🎧 **Listen again and fill in the blanks. You may use your notes to help you answer the questions.**

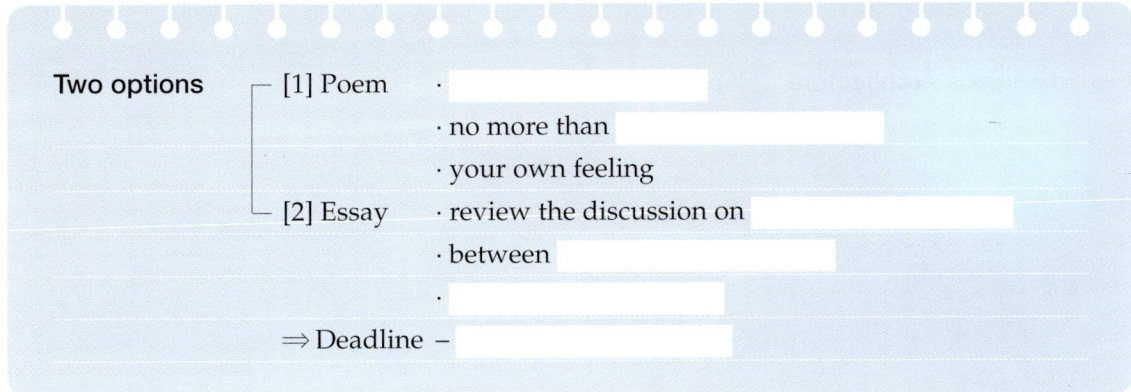

Two options ⎡ [1] Poem   · _____

                   · no more than _____

                   · your own feeling

        ⎣ [2] Essay · review the discussion on _____

                   · between _____

                   · _____

        ⇒ Deadline – _____

TOEFL Listening

VOLUME ◁))   HELP ?   OK ✓   NEXT ➡

HIDE TIME   00:00:00

🎧 **Listen to a talk in an architecture class then answer the questions.**

1 **Choose the correct statement for each item.**

	Temple	Abbey
It serves the community.		
It is more important to the royalty.		
It is designed to glorify the monarch.		
It is more practical in design.		

2 **According to the professor, which of the following is true?**

(A) This temple focuses on the whole community.

(B) This abbey is a community meeting place.

(C) They both serve the needs of the government.

(D) They are both important to France.

* cathedral 대성당   * select few 소수 정예주의

🎧 **Listen again and fill in the blanks. You may use your notes to help you answer the questions.**

Religious Architecture ┬ Abbey – · more _____
                       │   · for _____
                       │   · to glorify _____
                       └ Temple – · more _____
                                 · for _____
                                 · to benefit _____

 Exercise **4**

TOEFL Listening

VOLUME ◁)) HELP ? OK ✓ NEXT ➡

HIDE TIME 00:00:00

🎧 **Listen to a lecture in a science class then answer the questions.**

1 **Indicate which of the statements are the steps of tsunami.**

	Yes	No
Often earthquakes create tsunamis.		
Tides is one of the main causes of tsunamis.		
When the moon sets the sea suddenly creates massive waves.		
The surface of the ocean tries to copy the shape of the seafloor.		
Gravity returns the sea's surface back to its original shape.		

2 **According to the professor, what is tsunami?**
   (A) A very large wave that makes natural harbors
   (B) A very large wave that destroys natural harbors
   (C) A very large wave that fills harbors
   (D) A very large wave that comes into harbors

🎧 **Listen again and fill in the blanks. You may use your notes to help you answer the questions.**

Tsunami ┌ **Meaning** : [   ]
        └ **Process** : 1. [   ] occur
                        2. [   ] moves upward, sinks downwards
                        3. [   ] controls the sea's surface

Exercise 1

🎧 **Listen and fill in the blanks.**   (P=W, S=M)

Professor   How does one become President of the United States? First, party
members ① _____ candidate that will represent their party
② _____ general election. And then the people vote for
one candidate. However, when people cast a vote, ③_____
directly for an individual Presidential candidate. Voters ④_____
actually cast their vote for a group of people which we say is the Electoral
College.

Student   What's the Electoral College?

Professor   It is a system ⑤_____ as many electors ⑥_____
representatives and senators. And these electors cast their votes ⑦ _____
_____. Candidates who win this general election in
a state ⑧_____ state's electoral votes. If a candidate wins 270 or
more of the electoral votes then they become president.

|구문해설| **cast a vote** 투표하다   **representative** (미) 국회의원, 하원   **senator** 상원 의원   **win votes** 표를 얻다

- -

✔ **Check-up** for Expression

Complete the sentences using given words or phrases.

secure	presidential election	voters

1   He is a candidate for the next _____.

2   _____ elected Conservative candidates.

3   We need to _____ freedom of speech.

70

Exercise 2

🎧 **Listen and fill in the blanks.**   (S=W, P=M)

Student   What is our assignment for this class?

Professor   You have two options; you can ① _____ or compose a poem. If you write a poem ② _____ produce an original work that has the following elements: ③ _____; it's an expression of your own thoughts on grace; and is no more than 300 words long.

Student   Okay. What about the essay?

Professor   If you choose the essay option then I want to ④ _____ the current academic literature discussing grace; the paper must be between 2,000 and 2,500 words; and I also expect a full bibliography.

Student   ⑤ _____?

Professor   You have to ⑥ _____ before our last lesson.

Student   Wow! That's only two weeks away. ⑦ _____ the essay because it would take me ⑧ _____ to write a poem!

|구문해설| **either A or B** A 나 B 가운데 하나는   **grace** (신학) 하느님의 은총   **a review of ~** ~에 대한 논평[평가]   **bibliography** 관계 서적 목록   **hand in** 제출하다

✔ **Check-up** for Expression
- -

Complete the sentences using given words or phrases.

hand in	be required to	review of

1 You have to _____ your dictations right now.

2 You _____ get more than 80 points if you want to be recommended to the college.

3 The _____ the poem was very critical.

Exercise 3

🎧 **Listen and fill in the blanks.** (P=M, S=W)

Professor	Both the temple and the cathedral are two different types of religious architecture. Let's compare *The Temple of Srirangam* with *The Abbey of St. Denis*. The Srirangam temple was built for the people. ① _____ _____, through various rituals, it preserved moral values ② _____. The abbey, ③ _____, was focused on the select few, in this case, royalty.
Student	So the abbey in this case is more political rather than religious ④ _____.
Professor	What we're talking about here is the purpose for the architecture. One was ⑤ _____ the monarch but the other ⑥ _____ _____ the whole community.
Student	So then, that means... the temple serves society and the abbey primarily serves royalty?
Professor	Correct! The temple is more practical ⑦ _____, being a place for the people but the abbey ⑧ _____, respect and reverence for French royalty.

|구문해설| **serve as ~** ~의 역할을 하다 **abbey** 대수도원, 대성당 **the masses** 일반 대중, 서민 **in this case** 이러한 경우에 **focus on ~** ~에 초점을 맞추다 **glorify** 찬미하다, 영광을 찬양하다 **monarch** 군주, 제왕

✓ **Check-up** for Expression

Complete the sentences using given words or phrases.

focus on	rather than	serve as

1 He likes to read more current poems _____ the older, classical works.

2 Today's discussion will _____ methods for motivating employees.

3 We're looking for someone who can _____ an English teacher.

Exercise 4

🎧 **Listen and fill in the blanks.** (P=M)

Professor Sometimes gigantic waves ① _____ the oceans of the world. Some of you listening ② _____ this phenomenon by the name 'tidal wave', yes? But ③ _____ in modern times is the word 'tsunami', which means 'harbor wave.' Many scientists use this name because tides, ④ _____ the moon, do not create these massive waves. There are many different causes for tsunamis. They can be caused by landslides, volcanoes, eruptions and explosions of various kinds, but the most common cause is earthquakes. When earthquakes occur, part of the sea floor suddenly ⑤ _____ and part suddenly ⑥ _____. Immediately after this happens ⑦ _____ copy the shape of the sea floor. Gravity begins to take control and tries to return ⑧ _____ its original shape. As this occurs, the ragged sea begins to race outwards, and tries to ⑨ _____ again. At that moment a tsunami is born.

|구문해설| **gigantic** 거대한, 막대한 **occur in ~** ~에서 출현하다, ~에 존재하다 **by the name of ~** ~의 이름으로 **at that moment** 그 순간

✔ Check-up for Expression

Complete the sentences using given words or phrases.

occur in	caused by	return to

1 Mostly typhoons _____ the Pacific.

2 Sometimes people suffer from illness _____ the food they eat.

3 Salmon are known to _____ their birthplace to lay their eggs.

Write the meanings of the words or phrases in the blanks.

1	glorify		21	obtain
2	retain		22	fit
3	tribe		23	spine
4	upcoming		24	device
5	medical		25	representative
6	store		26	senator
7	long-term		27	bibliography
8	brief		28	abbey
9	explosion		29	encode
10	dominant		30	monarch
11	consist		31	the masses
12	opponent		32	win votes
13	origin		33	cast a vote
14	huge		34	either A or B
15	leading		35	hand in
16	retrieve		36	a great deal of ~
17	training		37	participate in ~
18	last		38	focus on ~
19	injure		39	serve as ~
20	organized		40	in this case

ORGANIZATION

OVERVIEW

Organization 문제는 강의나 대화에서 화자가 어떤 대상에 대해 설명하거나 자신의 요점을 효과적으로 전달하기 위해 어떤 말의 구조를 사용하고 있는지 묻는 문제이다. 화자가 배경을 설명하는지, 비교나 대조를 하는지, 예나 이유 등을 제시하는지 파악하는 것이 목적이다.

Question Types

How does the professor explain ~?
How does the professor clarify his point about ~?
How does the man develop the topic?
How does the woman describe ~?
In what order does the professor explain ~?

General Strategies

강의나 대화에서 핵심어(Key word)가 설명부분과 어떤 관계를 맺고 있는지 알아 본다. 화자가 말한 내용의 의미보다는 화자가 자신의 중심 생각을 전달하기 위해 어떤 내용을 어떤 방식으로 전달하고 있는지에 초점을 맞춰야 한다. 이 때 다음과 같은 Organizational signals를 파악하면 지문의 구조를 아는 데 도움이 될 수 있다.

(1) 예를 들 때,
   Let's say about ~ / For example ~ / To illustrate ~

(2) 이유/원인, 결과를 제시할 때
   Because (of) ~ / Due to the fact ~ / Thus ~ / Therefore ~ / For these reasons ~ / Consequently ~ / In conclusion ~

(3) 비교/대조할 때
   On the other hand ~ / On the contrary ~ / However[But] ~

(4) 증거를 제시할 때
   This shows ~ / This has been shown ~ / Based on ~

🎧 **Listen to a talk in a science class then answer the question.**

(P=M, S=W)

Professor	As we continue examining various weather phenomena, today let's discuss the tornado. Please open your books to page 32 where you can see photographs of tornadoes in action. Now take a close look and tell me where most of these photos have been taken.
Student	America?
Professor	Yes, that's right! Now why is it that America features so prominently in this textbook?
Student	The reason is because the United States experiences the most tornadoes.
Professor	Correct, it's the world's tornado capital with an average of 800 occurring each year. This is because they lack mountain ranges to block the dry air coming from Canada and the cool moisture originating from the Gulf of Mexico.

How does the professor explain tornadoes in America?

(A) By comparing with the number of tornado occurrences in Canada
(B) By explaining the features of American tornado in the text book
(C) By pointing out the reasons for the frequent tornadoes
(D) By explaining how the American tornadoes are formed

해설

미국이 매년 800 건이나 되는 토네이도가 발생하는 것은 캐나다에서 오는 건조한 공기와 멕시코 만에서 발생한 차가운 습기를 차단할 산악지대가 부족하기 때문이라며 그 이유를 설명하고 있다.

Word Preview

☐ demonstrate _____ ☐ link _____ ☐ genuine _____

 **Listen to the following and answer the question.**

How does the professor explain the media and its violence?

(A) By providing examples of children's violence

(B) By giving an example of a recent study

ORGANIZATION Choose the best answer to complete the outline of the passage below.

Study on Media by UCLA

1. violent _____
2. violent media
3. violence as _____   ≠ no link

• Children _____
  : _____ in incidents of children being violent

- - - - - - - - - - - - - - - - - - - -

(a) movies or films   (b) imitate what they see   (c) increase   (d) a joke

DICTATION 🎧 Listen again and fill in the blanks. (S=M, P=W)

Student   Incidents of children _____ increasing because of our media becoming more violent. Children _____ _____.

Professor   Actually, none of the studies _____ between them. Even if studies did demonstrate a link, _____ _____ what kind of media violence really matters. You might read the UCLA study. It demonstrates just how complex this issue has become. They had to cover so much: serious concerns on brutally violent movies or films: violent media that _____: and low level violence causing concern because _____. Which of these, if any, _____ concern, _____. There are no simple answers to this question.

✔ Check-up for Vocabulary

Choose the correct word in the box to complete the phrases.

imitate	violent	confirm	demonstrate	concern	genuine

1 safety _____

2 a(n) _____ quarrel

3 _____ an author's style

4 _____ a reservation

5 _____ the new theory

6 a(n) _____ Michelangelo's drawing

Word Preview

☐ High Renaissance _____   ☐ anatomy _____

🎧 **Listen to the following and answer the question.**

How does the professor explain about Raphael?

(A) By providing his life history from birth

(B) By listing important people in his era

ORGANIZATION Choose the best answer to complete the outline of the passage below.

Raphael

1483	1499	1504
· born in _____ · learn painting from _____	· meet _____	· move to _____ · study the works of _____

(a) Perugino   (b) Urbino   (c) Florence   (d) Michelangelo   (e) his father

DICTATION 🎧 **Listen again and fill in the blanks.**   (P=W)

Professor   _____ Raphael, one of the three major artists of the High Renaissance. He _____ Urbino in 1483. Raphael first learned about painting from his father, Giovanni Santi, _____ minor reputation. In 1499, he moved to Perugia in Umbria and _____ _____ Perugino. Raphael spent four years with Perugino _____ Perugino could teach him. At the end of the four years, in 1504, Raphael moved to Florence. There he studied the works of Michelangelo, Leonardo Da Vinci, and Fra Bartolommeo. He learned _____ by which he _____, shadow, the anatomy and dramatic representation.

* Perugino 움브리아 화파의 화가

✔ **Check-up** for Vocabulary
....

Choose the correct word in the box to complete the phrases.

born in	major	highly	reputation

1 _____ cities   3 have a good _____

2 _____ to a rich family   4 the _____ educated

CHAPTER 4

Word Preview

☐ fumes _____ ☐ exhaust _____ ☐ intensify _____

☐ electric power plant _____

 Listen to the following and answer the question.

How does the professor explain that acid rain is a result of air pollution?

(A) By giving examples of acid rain

(B) By explaining how acid rain is created

ORGANIZATION Choose the best answer to complete the outline of the passage below.

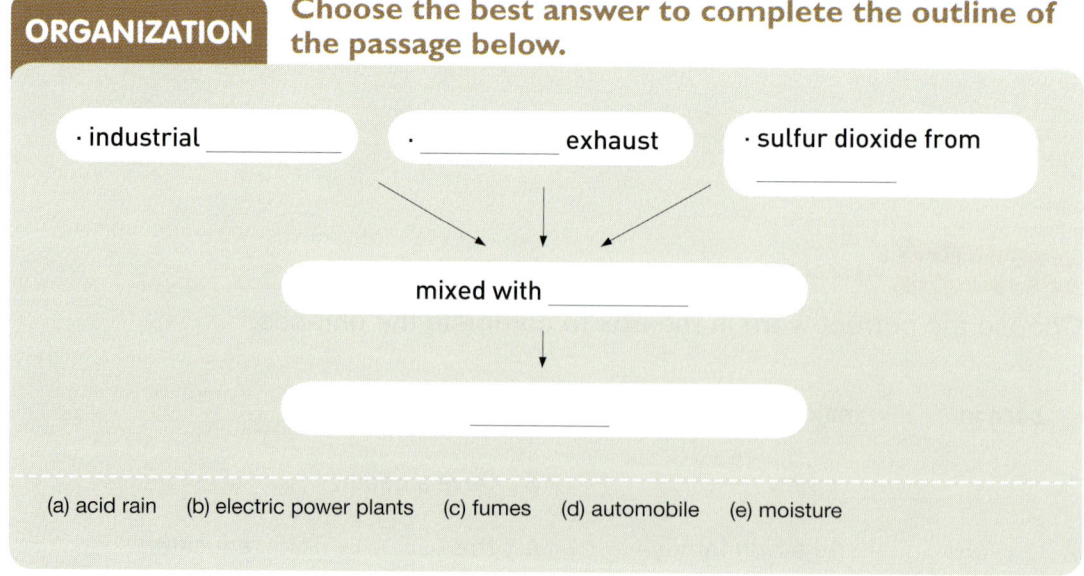

· industrial _____

· _____ exhaust

· sulfur dioxide from _____

→ mixed with _____

→ _____

(a) acid rain   (b) electric power plants   (c) fumes   (d) automobile   (e) moisture

DICTATION 🎧 Listen again and fill in the blanks. (P=M, S=W)

Professor	_____ air pollution, acid rain _____ _____ to our environment.
Student	How does air pollution become acid rain?
Professor	In some cases, acid rain is caused when industrial fumes _____ in the atmosphere and _____ _____ our rain fall. Another significant cause is automobile exhaust. Research _____ that sulfur dioxide from oil and nitrogen oxides produced from automobile engines _____ the problem.
Student	Maybe electric cars _____ the acid rain then?
Professor	Actually they _____ problems. Recent studies show that electric power plants release more than 20 million tons of sulfur dioxide each year.

* sulfur dioxide 아황산 가스   * nitrogen oxides 산화질소

✔ Check-up for Vocabulary

Choose the correct word in the box to complete the phrases.

industrial	automobile	intensify	reduce	release	significant

1 _____ risk

2 _____ waste

3 _____ accidents

4 _____ pressure

5 a(n) _____ event

6 _____ the author's new book

Word Preview

☐ artifact _____ ☐ restoration _____ ☐ anthropology _____

🎧 **Listen to the following and answer the question.**

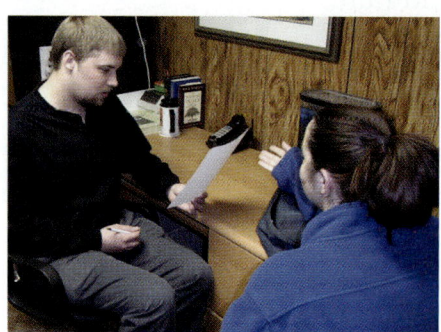

How does the professor help the student?

(A) By comparing the two classes

(B) By listing the good and bad points of his class

ORGANIZATION | Choose the best answer to complete the outline of the passage below.

Woman's Goal ---------- want to work for _____

Artifact Restoration – · _____

→ learn skill and experience

· _____ - only pass or fail

Anthropology – general, _____

(a) theoretical   (b) no exams or essays   (c) practical   (d) a museum

DICTATION 🎧 **Listen again and fill in the blanks.** (S=W, P=M)

Student _____ another class and I'm trying to decide on the best choice, Artifact Restoration or Anthropology.

Professor What is it you want to _____?

Student _____ a museum when I graduate.

Professor Ah! Then, my class is definitely the best choice for you. Anthropology is general and theoretical, whereas this class is _____. You'll learn the skills you need through lectures and work experience in actual museums.

Student Sounds good, but _____ a lot more work?

Professor Actually no! Because it's a practical course there are no essays or exams. We evaluate you progressively _____ for the museums. It's simply _____.

✔ **Check-up** **for Vocabulary**

Choose the correct word in the box to complete the phrases.

achieve	general	degree	specific	practical	evaluate

1 _____ victory

2 _____ English

3 the _____ public

4 get a high _____

5 _____ needs

6 _____ the quality of the work

■ Exercise 1

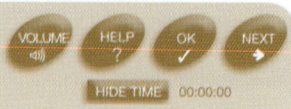

TOEFL Listening

VOLUME · HELP ? · OK ✓ · NEXT →

HIDE TIME 00:00:00

🎧 **Listen to a lecture in a music class then answer the questions.**

1 How does the professor introduce Baroque music?

(A) By explaining what the word Baroque means

(B) By asking some questions about Baroque music

(C) By giving some examples of Baroque music

(D) By explaining what is different about Baroque music

2 According to the professor, what are TWO differences between Renaissance music and Baroque music? Choose TWO answers.

(A) The way instruments are used

(B) The number of singers

(C) The way singers are used

(D) The origins of a word

🎧 **Listen again and fill in the blanks. You may use your notes to help you answer the questions.**

> **Baroque Music** (*"a pearl in irregular shape in Portuguese"*)
> · instrument :
> · soloist :
> **Renaissance Music**
> · instrument :
> · soloist :

 **Exercise 2**

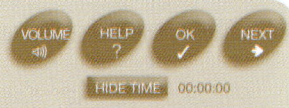
TOEFL Listening

VOLUME   HELP   OK   NEXT

HIDE TIME   00:00:00

🎧 **Listen to a lecture in an architecture class then answer the questions.**

1 How does the professor explain Gothic architecture?

(A) By explaining its historical background
(B) By showing some slides of Gothic archicture
(C) By providing several famous Gothic theories
(D) By comparing with Romanesque architecture

2 Which of the following is NOT mentioned about both styles of architecture?

(A) The number of windows
(B) The purpose of the wall
(C) The purpose of the building
(D) The way of preventing light entering the building

🎧 **Listen again and fill in the blanks. You may use your notes to help you answer the questions.**

```
┌ Gothic Architecture      · purpose :  artistic
│                          · feature  :  ① wall - _____
│                                         ② windows - _____
│                                              → stained glass
└ Romanesque Architecture  · purpose :  _____
                           · feature  :  ① wall - _____
                                          ② windows - _____
                                               → add wall paintings/mosaics
```

 # Exercise **3**

🎧 **Listen to a lecture in a medical class then answer the questions.**

1 How does the professor explain the nervous system?

(A) By classifying it into two parts

(B) By explaining its working process

(C) By discussing its effects on the body

(D) By emphasizing its importance

2 Which of the following is NOT true? Choose TWO answers.

(A) The PNS is more intelligent than the CNS.

(B) The PNS tells the CNS what to do.

(C) The PNS takes instructions from the CNS.

(D) The PNS collects information for the CNS.

* central nervous system 중추 신경계   * peripheral nervous system 말초 신경계

🎧 **Listen again and fill in the blanks. You may use your notes to help you answer the questions.**

Nervous System ┬ **CNS**

· consists : _____

· work : _____

  → integrating, processing, coordinating

└ **PNS**

· consists : _____

· work : _____

  → carries motor commands to peripheral tissues and systems

Exercise 4

TOEFL Listening VOLUME 🔊 HELP ? OK ✓ NEXT ➡

HIDE TIME 00:00:00

🎧 **Listen to a conversation between a student and a librarian then answer the questions.**

1 How does the man help the woman?
(A) By pointing out the possible cause of the problem
(B) By showing the right process
(C) By contrasting it with his work
(D) By emphasizing the different functions of computers

2 Why does the man suggest to use his computer?
(A) Because his computer is the newest one.
(B) Because his computer's drive is larger than the woman's.
(C) Because the computer the woman is using is out of order.
(D) Because the computer the woman is using is off-line.

* mirror site [컴퓨터] (인터넷의) 미러 사이트 《특정 사이트의 백업·혼잡 회피를 위해 설치》

🎧 **Listen again and fill in the blanks. You may use your notes to help you answer the questions.**

Problem with Downloading File
– _____ (did not work)
– _____ (did not work)
· **Cause :** Huge amount of _____
→ take up a lot of _____
· **Solution :** _____

Exercise 1

🎧 **Listen and fill in the blanks.**

(P=W)

Professor What are ① _____ Renaissance music and the 17th century style of music called Baroque? Does anyone know? ② _____, so I'll tell you. But, first, what is Baroque? The word Baroque comes from the Portuguese noun 'barroco' ③ _____ 'a pearl of irregular shape.' The modern use of the word Baroque is ④ _____, a culture ⑤ _____ _____, confident and brilliant. Now the differences are ⑥ _____ _____ instruments and the introduction of soloists. Baroque uses instruments to produce music. This music complements but ⑦ _____ _____ with their voice. In the case of the Renaissance, if instruments ⑧ _____ they simply copied the singer's sound. The other difference, ⑨ _____, was the introduction of solos. In the Renaissance period, all sacred music ⑩ _____ _____. In the Baroque period, soloists were used.

|구문해설| **irregular** 불규칙한, 변칙적인 **brilliant** 훌륭한, 멋진 **soloist** 독주자, 독창자 **complement** ~의 보완이 되다 **if ~ at all** 같은 값이면 **sacred music** 종교 음악

✓ **Check-up** for Expression

Complete the sentences using given words or phrases.

come from	performed by	in the case of

1 All data _____ the main server.

2 You'd better reboot the computer _____ a transfer error.

3 Almost all the work in his section was _____ robots.

Exercise 2

🎧 **Listen and fill in the blanks.** (P=M)

Professor   Today we are going to study Gothic architecture. ① _____
_____ some of its differences to Romanesque styles of architecture, which
we studied last class. Romanesque architecture is designed more ② _____
_____ than for any artistic sense. The walls of Romanesque
cathedrals ③ _____ to resist attacks by invaders. Gothic, on
the other hand, ④ _____, focusing more ⑤ _____
_____. You may remember that due to the thickness of the walls
Romanesque cathedrals have very few windows. To brighten these
cathedrals, ⑥ _____ wall paintings and mosaics. Whereas
Gothic makes great use of many stained glass windows ⑦ _____
_____ creating a peaceful interior. Obviously these styles had
very different purposes ⑧ _____.

|구문해설| **Gothic** 고딕 양식의   **Romanesque** 로마네스크 식의   **protective** 보호하는, 방어하는   **attack by ~** ~에 의한 공격
invader 침략자, 침입자   **due to ~** ~ 때문에, ~에 기인하는   **make use of ~** ~을 이용하다

✔ **Check-up** **for Expression**
- -
Complete the sentences using given words or phrases.

make use of	designed for	due to

1   _____ the flood, the farmers have had poor crops this year.

2   This is the track _____ the model car race.

3   It's very important for you to _____ your own experience.

Dictation for Exercise

Exercise 3

🎧 **Listen and fill in the blanks.** (P=M)

Professor Now we ① _____ the nervous system. ② _____ _____ to memorize, ③ _____ its two parts; the central nervous system and the peripheral nervous system. Use the initials CNS and PNS in your notes. ④ _____ as the information provider and the former as the information processor. The PNS communicates information, and the CNS ⑤ _____ as a result of the information received. The CNS ⑥ _____ the brain and the spinal cord. ⑦ _____ integrating, processing, and coordinating sensory data and motor commands. The CNS ⑧ _____ _____ higher learning, performing such functions as intelligence, memory, learning, and emotion. The PNS includes ⑨ _____ _____ the CNS. The PNS carries motor commands to the peripheral tissues and systems.

|구문해설| **move on to ~** ~로 옮기다   **nervous system** 신경 계통   **split ~ into...** ~을 …로 나누다[쪼개다]   **spinal** 척수의, 척추의
tissue (생물) 조직

✔ Check-up for Expression

Complete the sentences using given words or phrases.

as a result of	responsible for	split into

1 The class was _____ two by the issue.

2 The report claims that media is _____ increases in children violence.

3 The cost of the product rose twofold _____ high demand.

92

Exercise 4

🎧 **Listen and fill in the blanks.**   (S=W, L=M)

Student   Ugh! Not again!

Librarian   Hey! Shush…remember it's a library!

Student   Sorry, ①_____ I've tried downloading this file.

Librarian   What is it?

Student   A research paper. Every time I try, the download fails to complete.

Librarian   Have you tried ②_____, or using a mirror site?

Student   Yes, I tried both, but ③_____ download.

Librarian   Hmmm… ④_____ and let me try. Ah! I see the problem. The file's too large for this drive.

Student   Really? But it's a text document so ⑤_____.

Librarian   Actually it is because it has a huge amount of high quality images which always ⑥_____. You'd better use my work computer. Its main drive is larger.

|구문해설| **refresh** [컴퓨터] (장치의 내용을) 재생하다   **take up** (공간 등을) 차지하다, 잡다

✔ **Check-up** for Expression

Complete the sentences using given words or phrases.

move over	take up	fail to

1 The meeting would _____ more space than expected.

2 He never _____ remember a person's name.

3 Please _____ these books for me.

Vocabulary Review

Write the meanings of the words or phrases in the blanks.

1	demonstrate		21	artifact	
2	link		22	intensify	
3	genuine		23	anthropology	
4	imitate		24	achieve	
5	Gothic		25	general	
6	confirm		26	degree	
7	concern		27	specific	
8	refresh		28	practical	
9	anatomy		29	evaluate	
10	invader		30	irregular	
11	major		31	brilliant	
12	highly		32	soloist	
13	reputation		33	complement	
14	fumes		34	protective	
15	exhaust		35	take up	
16	restoration		36	attack by ~	
17	industrial		37	born in ~	
18	automobile		38	due to ~	
19	reduce		39	make use of ~	
20	release		40	move on to ~	

INFERENCE / STANCE

OVERVIEW

Inference는 화자가 말한 내용을 토대로 또 다른 사실이나 결론을 추론해 내는 것을 말하며 Stance는 화자의 생각이나 입장을 유추하는 것을 말한다. 이들 유형은 특히 Replay Question이라고 하여, 전체의 일부를 다시 들려 주고 그 부분에 나타난 의미, 또는 화자의 입장/태도를 묻기도 한다.

Question Types

What can be inferred from the lecture?
What will the man probably do next?
How does the woman feel about ~?
What is the man's opinion of ~?
What does the woman mean when she says this:
What does the professor imply when she says this:

General Strategies

1 추론하기 (Inference)

추론은 화자가 강의나 대화에서 언급된 내용만을 근거로 하여야 하며 주어진 정보가 아닌 상식적인 내용이나 언급된 사실의 반복, 또는 지나친 억측은 피해야 한다.

2 입장/태도 파악하기 (Stance)

화자가 언급하고 있는 내용에 대해 어떤 입장이나 태도를 취하고 있는지를 파악한다. 이 때 화자가 그 말을 하게 된 이유나 배경까지 파악하면 보다 정확한 답을 찾을 수 있다. 같은 말이나 표현이라도 그 말을 한 상황에 따라 긍정적인지 부정적인지, 신뢰하는지 의심하는지, 회의적인지 적극적인지 등이 달라질 수 있음도 유념하자.

VOLUME 🔊 HELP ? OK ✓ NEXT →

HIDE TIME 00:00:00

🎧 **Listen to a talk in a math class then answer the question.**

(P=M, S=W)

Professor	When thinking of the concepts of math and music, do you see any connection?
Student	No, not really.
Professor	That's what most people say. In reality, mathematics has a tremendous effect on music. Pythagoras was the first to discover the mathematical basis for music. He observed that there was a connection between the length of a string and the pitch of its vibrating note.
Student	But what does that have to do with math?
Professor	Well, by conducting experiments, Pythagoras discovered that the shorter a string, the higher the pitch or frequency was. So when he shortened the string to half of its original length, the note sounded higher. He also found that an octave is obtained by shortening the string to one half of its original length, thereby doubling the frequency. Now that's math!

What does the professor imply when he says this: 🎧

(A) People believe that math has a great effect on music.

(B) People do not think math is a practical subject.

(C) People do not see any connection between math and music.

(D) People discovered that math is very helpful to understand music theory.

해설

수학과 음악과의 관련성을 묻는 교수의 질문에 학생은 '관련성이 없는 것 같다'고 대답한다. 교수는 대부분의 사람들이 학생과 같은 생각을 하고 있다고 말하고 있다.

Word Preview

☐ slave trade _____   ☐ racist _____   ☐ willing to _____
☐ enrichment _____

🎧 **Listen to the following and answer the question.**

What can be inferred from the lecture?

(A) Some African nations sold off their people to raise money.

(B) The African slave trade caused political struggles between Spain and Portugal.

ORGANIZATION

Choose the best answer to complete the outline of the passage below.

African Slave Trade

Background : in search of _____

Spain
• need _____

Portugal
• consider Africans to be _____

Some African nations
• willing to participate in _____

(a) cheap workers   (b) goods   (c) the trade   (d) gold

DICTATION 🎧 **Listen again and fill in the blanks.** (P=M)

> Professor In the 1400's, Portugal and Spain _____ the
> ultimate prize of exploration – gold! Even though, from
> an historical perspective, the African slave trade _____
> _____, it was actually _____ the economic
> benefits that _____. The Spaniards needed cheap
> workers in America _____ to find the gold.
> Portugal got involved with this because they _____
> _____ to use these slaves _____
> _____ Spain. It should also _____ some African
> nations themselves were _____ participate
> in the trade. The slaves' skin color or ethnic background was
> not that important. The focus was on the opportunity for
> economic enrichment.

✔ **Check-up** **for Vocabulary**

Choose the correct word in the box to complete the phrases.

ultimate	motivate	involve	opportunity	trade	participate in

1 _____ in furs

2 _____ a lot of work

3 equal _____

4 _____ a debate

5 _____ goal in life

6 _____ employees by rewarding them

Word Preview

□ germ _____ □ decompose _____ □ organism _____
□ decay _____ □ vaccination _____

🎧 **Listen to the following and answer the question.**

What is the professor's attitude towards bacteria?

(A) She thinks that bacteria has a lot of bad effects.

(B) She points out that bacteria has lots of helpful uses.

ORGANIZATION **Choose the best answer to complete the outline of the passage below.**

People mostly think bacteria _____ or disease

Benefit
· _____ waste materials
· produce _____
   → _____ against bacteria

Damage
· _____ in humans

(a) cause a disease (b) germs (c) fight a disease (d) decompose (e) antibodies

DICTATION 🎧 Listen again and fill in the blanks. (P=W)

Professor   When people think of bacteria, _____ germs and disease. Most of us, however, _____ the fact that there are literally thousands of bacteria _____ _____. One of the good things that _____ _____ decompose waste materials, _____, it helps to _____. Without these special bacteria, the remains of dead organisms and plants _____ _____ and pretty soon, there would be garbage everywhere! Actually, although bacteria can cause disease in humans, it can also _____. For example, _____ dead bacteria into the body, the body produces the same antibodies that it _____ _____ live bacteria. This process is called vaccination.

✔ Check-up for Vocabulary

Choose the correct word in the box to complete the phrases.

germ	ignore	maintain	balance	inject	protect

1 _____ a good condition   4 _____ medicine into a vein

2 an influenza _____   5 _____ eyes from the sun

3 _____ their opinions   6 a(n) _____ of mind and body

Word Preview

☐ fund _____   ☐ health insurance _____   ☐ discrimination _____

🎧 **Listen to the following and answer the question.**

What does the man mean when he says this: 🎧

(A) People need to pay more tax to help poor people.

(B) It is not fair to make people to pay more taxes.

ORGANIZATION **Choose the best answer to complete the outline of the passage below.**

Health Care Insurance

Goal : give _____ to all people
Controversial : can lead to more taxes

↓   ↓

Situation 1   **Situation 2**

Poor people   **Many people**
· can't get _____   · have to _____
· _____, or not having a
  job that provides health insurance

(a) health insurance coverage   (b) pay more taxes   (c) proper health care   (d) a lack of money

DICTATION 🎧 **Listen again and fill in the blanks.**   (P=W, S1=W, P=M)

Professor	Government Funded Health Care is a health insurance plan _____ the government that would give health insurance coverage _____ discrimination. What do you think about this?
Student 1	I think poor people would like it but _____ _____.
Professor	You have a point. Numerous individuals in the United States _____ because of _____ _____ money or not having a job that provides health insurance. Having such a plan would allow these people to _____. The question is whether or not the U.S. _____.
Student 2	I think we have _____ for the health care. I think they should provide more jobs instead.

✔ **Check-up** **for Vocabulary**

Choose the correct word in the box to complete the phrases.

numerous	proper	lack	provide	insurance	tax

1 life _____

2 _____ of skill

3 a(n) _____ army

4 take a(n) _____ step

5 _____ 24-hour service

6 impose a heavy _____

Word Preview

☐ flu _____ ☐ put off _____ ☐ delay _____

🎧 **Listen to the following and answer the question.**

How does the man probably feel?

(A) He is worried about not studying.

(B) He is relieved that he has more time.

ORGANIZATION

Choose the best answer to complete the outline of the passage below.

How does the man feel?

" _____ "

: _____ because of the flu

: doesn't know _____ the final exam is

→

" _____ "

: Professor _____ for a week

: has more time to review

- -

(a) relieved   (b) when and where   (c) missed his class   (d) worried   (e) put the exam off

DICTATION 🎧 **Listen again and fill in the blanks.** (S1=M, S2=W)

Student 1	Hey there. Did you go to the last class?
Student 2	Yeah, why?
Student 1	Oh, I _____ it and I don't know _____ the final exam is.
Student 2	Why did you miss the class?
Student 1	_____. I was so sick I couldn't even study.
Student 2	Are you feeling better now?
Student 1	Yes, much better. Thanks.
Student 2	Well… the exam is in the main hall, but… actually… the professor said _____, so don't worry too much.
Student 1	So… _____. That's great! I'll have _____ _____!
Student 2	Yeah, me too. Want to be my study partner?
Student 1	Sure.

✓ **Check-up** **for Vocabulary**

Choose the correct word in the box to complete the phrases.

miss	put off	delay	review

1 _____ the lessons   3 because of a traffic _____

2 _____ an opportunity   4 _____ an appointment

 **Exercise 1**

TOEFL Listening

VOLUME 🔊 HELP ? OK ✓ NEXT ➡

HIDE TIME 00:00:00

🎧 **Listen to a discussion in a law class then answer the questions.**

1 **What is the woman's opinion of the use of rhetoric?**
   (A) She thinks that that it is a bad thing to use.
   (B) She thinks that lawyers need it more now.
   (C) She thinks it is okay to use it for good reasons.
   (D) She thinks that lawyers who use it are dishonest.

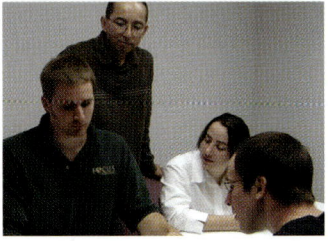

2 **According to the professor, what is rhetoric?**
   (A) The ability to tell really good stories
   (B) The ability to cover the truth
   (C) The ability to convince people
   (D) The ability to prove the truth

🎧 **Listen again and fill in the blanks. You may use your notes to help you answer the questions.**

What is a rhetoric in a trial

:

→ Lawyers use _____ to persuade the jury

→ _____ will sometimes make decisions based on

_____ , not on _____

· Opinion 1 – _____

· Opinion 2 – _____

Exercise 2

TOEFL Listening

VOLUME ◁))   HELP ?   OK ✓   NEXT →

HIDE TIME   00:00:00

🎧 **Listen to a talk in a psychology class then answer the questions.**

1 What does the professor mean when she says this : 🎧

(A) Stress can be very useful for us.

(B) Stress can never be avoided by physicians.

(C) Stress makes everyone who has it very sick.

(D) Stress is something people must learn to live with.

2 Which of the following is NOT mentioned as the cause of stress?

(A) Meeting business deadlines

(B) Social issues like pollution or crime

(C) Relationships between friends

(D) Concerns about grades

🎧 **Listen again and fill in the blanks. You may use your notes to help you answer the questions.**

What stress is : _____

What causes stress :

     • For teenagers – _____

     • For adults   – _____

     • For everyone – _____

How to deal with stress : Learn how to live with these situations

CHAPTER 5

TOEFL Listening   VOLUME 🔊   HELP ?   OK ✓   NEXT ➡

HIDE TIME   00:00:00

🎧 **Listen to a talk in a biology class then answer the questions.**

1 **What can be inferred when the professor says this:** 🎧

(A) That one day there may be a breakthrough.

(B) That one day cloning may no longer be worthwhile.

(C) That one day cloning may prove to be a good thing.

(D) That one day there will be no more controversy regarding cloning.

2 **Listen to part of the talk again.** 🎧

What does the professor imply when he says this: 🎧

(A) Most people do not like cloning.

(B) More people need to accept cloning.

(C) Some arguments are based on false ideas.

(D) Most arguments are very popular myths.

* artificial insemination 인공 수정   * embryo 태아

🎧 **Listen again and fill in the blanks. You may use your notes to help you answer the questions.**

Cloning - Controversial, but may turn out to be _____ like artificial insemination

· **Protesters believe cloning is**

– _____ of an existing human being

– _____

· **What cloning really is**

– only produces _____

– have unique experience

**Exercise4**

TOEFL Listening

VOLUME HELP OK NEXT
  ?   ✓

HIDE TIME 00:00:00

🎧 **Listen to a conversation between a student and a librarian then answer the questions.**

1 Listen to part of the conversation again. 🎧

Why does the woman say this: 🎧

(A) To tell him that she has some information that might help

(B) To tell him that he should believe she can help him

(C) To tell him that she feels bad about his situation

(D) To tell him that she is worried about her paper, too

2 What will the man probably do next?

(A) He will go to the woman's house.

(B) He will go to the library to find more information.

(C) He will ask his professor for more time.

(D) He will ask her professor about the video.

CHAPTER 5

🎧 **Listen again and fill in the blanks. You may use your notes to help you answer the questions.**

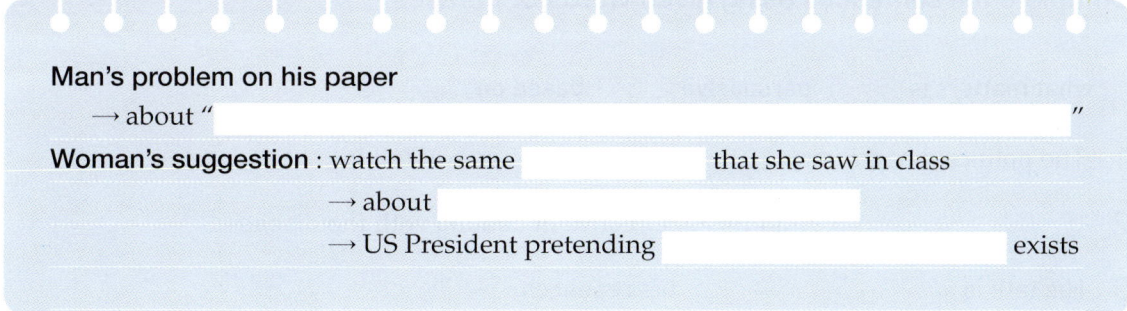

Man's problem on his paper
→ about " _____ "

Woman's suggestion : watch the same _____ that she saw in class
→ about _____
→ US President pretending _____ exists

Dictation for Exercise

Exercise 1

🎧 **Listen and fill in the blanks.** (P=M, S1=M, S2=W)

Professor ① _____, lawyers often use rhetoric. Rhetoric, you know, ② _____ _____. They sometimes use information ③ _____ _____ the case. Often a jury will not decide a case ④ _____ _____ but on the rhetoric. What do you think?

Student 1 Guilt and innocence, getting to the truth, is not the issue these days. Rhetoric serves only one purpose: ⑤ _____. Honest lawyers ⑥ _____ that way.

Student 2 I'm sorry but I can't agree with you. The use of rhetoric is ⑦ _____ _____. What matters is why you use this skill. If my client is innocent, but I don't have the evidence to prove it, then ⑧ _____ using rhetoric. If the result is good then it doesn't matter if the complete truth ⑨ _____.

|구문해설| **trial** 재판, 공판   **rhetoric** 웅변, 수사학   **jury** 배심(원단)   **guilt** 유죄, 범죄   **obscure** 가리다, 은폐하다   **neither A nor B** A도 B도 아니다

✔ Check-up for Expression

Complete the sentences using given words or phrases.

what matters is	persuasive	based on

1 The politician had a very _____ way of talking.

2 _____ that this is effective in dealing with the disease.

3 His talk is _____ his research.

110

Exercise 2

🎧 **Listen and fill in the blanks.** (P=W, S=M)

Professor Today's lecture ① _____ : what it is, what causes it, and ② _____ _____ . Stress affects everyone and everything. One way of describing stress is nervousness, anxiety, mental discomfort, or pressure. There are many things that cause stress. Any ideas?

Student I sometimes ③ _____ . *(Everyone laughs.)*

Professor Popularity, friends, relationships, and looks are often stressful for teenagers. However, adults ④ _____ different kinds of stress such as meeting business deadlines. But everybody ⑤ _____ stress ⑥ _____ wars, pollution, or crime. It is important to learn how to live with these situations because it's ⑦ _____ _____ life without encountering them. Physicians ⑧ _____ that diseases ⑨ _____ are more likely to happen to people with very busy lives.

Student Let's all go home and ⑩ _____ ! *(More laughs.)*

|구문해설| **tend to ~** ~하는 경향이 있다   **face** 직면하다, 마주하다   **get through** 극복하다, 끝내다   **be likely to happen** (일이) 일어날 것 같다

✔ Check-up for Expression

Complete the sentences using given words or phrases.

tend to	be likely to	get through

1 It _____ rain this evening.

2 We had to _____ many difficulties to finish the work.

3 People _____ change brands frequently.

Exercise 3

🎧 **Listen and fill in the blanks.**   (P=M, S=W)

Professor Science ① _____ controversy. For example, breakthroughs ② _____ artificial insemination ③ _____ _____ in the past. However, time has proved that such advances are worthwhile. ④ _____ with cloning. What do you think about this?

Student Well... I always ⑤ _____ .

Professor Many people feel that way. But protesters who feel that cloning ⑥ _____ don't really understand it. In fact, many arguments against human cloning are misconceptions. One popular myth is that people think cloning technology can produce ⑦ _____ _____ an existing human being. This is not true. Cloning technology can only produce a cloned embryo and the developed child ⑧ _____ _____ . People also think that a clone will be both behaviorally and physically ⑨ _____ . This also is not true.

|구문해설| **breakthrough** (과학 등의) 큰 약진, 새로운 발견   **protester** 항의하는 사람, 이의 제기자   **ban** 금지하다, 반대하다 **misconception** 잘못된 생각, 오해   **identical to ~** ~와 꼭 같은, 일치하는

✔ **Check-up** for Expression
....
Complete the sentences using given words or phrases.

ban	identical to	fill with

1 The girl _____ amazement.

2 This style is _____ none.

3 Many people agree that nuclear tests should be _____ .

Exercise 4

🎧 **Listen and fill in the blanks.**   (S1=M, S2=W)

Student 1 Oh, man! This is so hard!

Student 2 What's wrong?

Student 1 ① _____ this essay.

Student 2 What's your topic?

Student 1 'How has fear become ② _____ in modern American politics.'

Student 2 Really? ③ _____, but just this morning our class watched an excellent BBC video ④ _____. It's about the US President and his use of fear. ⑤ _____ there's a global terror organization. We get very afraid, and so then we give him all the power he wants.

Student 1 Ah… I get it now. He ⑥ _____ giving him power ⑦ _____ protection from things that doesn't exist. Just like those weapons of mass destruction ⑧ _____. Hmmm… I wonder if your professor took that video home or left it in the classroom.

|구문해설| **figure out** 이해하다; 해결하다 **pretend** ~인 체하다, 가장하다 **scare** 위협하다, 겁나게 하다 **in return for ~** ~의 답례로, ~의 회답으로 **wonder if ~** ~인지 아닌지 모르다

✔ **Check-up** for Expression

Complete the sentences using given words or phrases.

figure out	in return for	wonder if

1 Did you _____ what was wrong?

2 I _____ it's a good idea for the project.

3 What shall I give you _____ your help?

Vocabulary Review

Write the meanings of the words or phrases in the blanks.

1	germ	_____	21	scare	_____
2	slave trade	_____	22	health insurance	_____
3	jury	_____	23	discrimination	_____
4	motivate	_____	24	breakthrough	_____
5	opportunity	_____	25	protester	_____
6	decay	_____	26	ban	_____
7	vaccination	_____	27	misconception	_____
8	guilt	_____	28	face	_____
9	organism	_____	29	racist	_____
10	inject	_____	30	decompose	_____
11	fund	_____	31	wonder if ~	_____
12	flu	_____	32	willing to ~	_____
13	delay	_____	33	participate in ~	_____
14	trial	_____	34	put off	_____
15	maintain	_____	35	tend to ~	_____
16	obscure	_____	36	get through ~	_____
17	enrichment	_____	37	be likely to ~	_____
18	ultimate	_____	38	identical to ~	_____
19	trade	_____	39	figure out	_____
20	pretend	_____	40	in return for ~	_____

FUNCTION

OVERVIEW

Function-Purpose 문제는 화자가 어떤 말을 하는 이유나 목적, 즉 그 말이 하는 기능을 말한다. 강의나 대화에서 화자가 한 말의 의도나 의미를 묻기도 하므로, 앞뒤 문맥을 파악하여 말에 나타나는 억양이나 어조를 통해 속에 담긴 의미까지 파악하도록 하자.

Question Types

Why does the professor say ~?
Why does the professor mention ~?
Why does the man say this:
Listen to part of the lecture again. What does the professor mean when he says this:

General Strategies

화자가 어떤 것을 언급한 이유를 물어보거나, 전체의 일부를 다시 들려 준 후 화자가 그 말을 한 이유를 물어본다. 때문에 화자가 말한 것의 목적이나 동기를 생각하도록 한다. 예를 들어, 그 말이 사과를 하려는 것인지, 불평을 하려는 것인지, 제안을 하려는 것인지 등을 따지는 것인데, 이 때 화자의 Tone이나 Intonation을 듣고 의도된 의미를 파악하는 것이 중요하다.

Purpose의 예
   To emphasize / imply / indicate ~
   To prove / give a reason for ~
   To compare / contrast ~
   To encourage / persuade ~
   To recommend / suggest / advice ~
   To complain / appologize ~
   To give an opinion / agree / disagree ~
   To request / invite ~

SAMPLE

🎧 **Listen to a talk in a psychology class then answer the question.**

(P=W, S=M)

Professor	Skinner's entire system is based on operant conditioning. An organism bounces around the world until it encounters a stimulus that strengthens or weakens the behavior that produced it. This stimulus has the effect of increasing or decreasing the behavior that just occurred. This is operant conditioning: a behavior is followed by a consequence, and that consequence affects the organism's behavior in the future. Is that clear?
Student	Uh, well... I don't think so.
Professor	All right, then. Imagine a rat in a special cage that has a pedal on one wall: when pressed, the pedal releases a food pellet into the cage. The rat is bouncing around the cage, doing whatever it is that rats do, when he accidentally presses the pedal and, like magic, a food pellet falls into the cage! In no time at all, the rat is furiously peddling away to get more food pellets.

Why does the professor mention a rat in a cage?

(A) To exemplify operant conditioning

(B) To suggest an idea for a experiment

(C) To show how a rat behave when it is kept in a cage

(D) To explain a special role of a rat in operant conditioning experiment

해설

학생이 작동적 조건 형성에 대한 설명을 제대로 이해하지 못하자, 교수는 학생의 이해를 돕기 위해 그 같은 사례를 다룬 한 실험을 예로 들고 있다.

Word Preview

☐ pilot _____ ☐ questionnaire _____ ☐ conduct _____

Listen to the following and answer the question.

Why does the professor say this: 🎧

(A) To show that she thinks that there is no problem

(B) To show that she doesn't understand the problem

ORGANIZATION — Choose the best answer to complete the outline of the passage below.

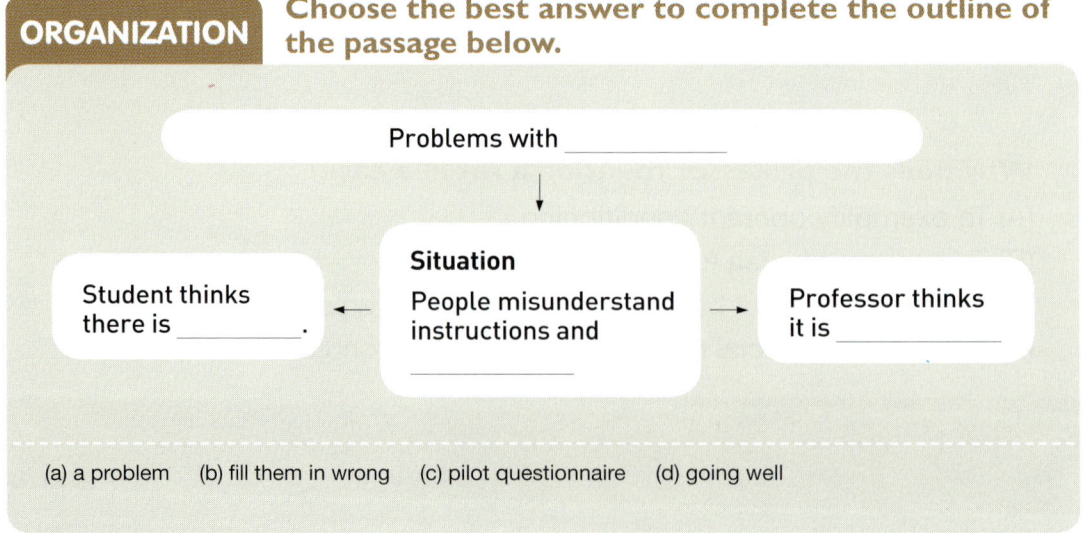

Problems with _____

↓

Situation
People misunderstand instructions and _____

Student thinks there is _____. ←

→ Professor thinks it is _____

(a) a problem   (b) fill them in wrong   (c) pilot questionnaire   (d) going well

DICTATION 🎧 **Listen again and fill in the blanks.**   (S=M, P=W)

Student	Excuse me, Professor. _____ my experiment. Could you advise me?
Professor	_____ the problem?
Student	Well, I'm having a few problems with my pilot questionnaire. People are misunderstanding some of the instructions and _____.
Professor	So... what's the problem? *(Thinking it is going well.)*
Student	Well, I... _____. People are filling them in wrong.
Professor	Well, _____ conducting a pilot study — _____ and what doesn't work before you give the questionnaire to more people. If there are problems, you _____ before doing the final questionnaire. Do you need help to correct these problems?
Student	Oh, I see... no, it's okay, I can do that. Thanks, Professor.

✔ **Check-up** for Vocabulary

Choose the correct word in the box to complete the phrases.

experiment	questionnaire	instruction	pilot	fix	correct

1 _____ a machine

2 _____ errors

3 a(n) _____ study

4 a chemical _____

5 conduct a(n) _____

6 follow the _____

Word Preview

☐ rain forest _____ ☐ species _____ ☐ resource _____

🎧 **Listen to the following and answer the question.**

Why does the professor mention malaria?

(A) To give an example of a disease that can be cured with medicine found in the rain forest

(B) To point out that some of the plants in the rain forest are the cause of some disease

---

ORGANIZATION **Choose the best answer to complete the outline of the passage below.**

Rain Forest

— **Problem**

being destroyed at an alarming rate

— **Importance**

(1) home for _____

(2) _____ :

→ _____ are found in rain forests

e.g. quinine effective for treating _____

(a) malaria   (b) medicines   (c) 50% of all species   (d) a vital health resource

DICTATION 🎧 Listen again and fill in the blanks. (P=M)

Professor Our rain forests _____ an alarming rate. Even though there are no rain forests in most countries, still rain forests greatly _____ around the world. Rain forests are the home of about _____.

It's also a vital health resource so they must be protected _____ all people. Many medicines are found in the rain forests which treat common diseases. You know what malaria is, right? It's a disease that _____ _____ quinine, _____ the cinchona tree in Peru.

* quinine 키니네 제(劑), 염산[황산] 키니네 《말라리아 특효약》
* cinchona 기나 나무, 기나피 제제(製劑)

✔ Check-up for Vocabulary

Choose the correct word in the box to complete the phrases.

rain forest	destroy	species	resource	medicine	common

1 liquid _____

2 a natural _____

3 a tropical _____

4 endangered _____

5 _____ the building

6 a(n) _____ language

Word Preview

☐ prescription _____ ☐ alter _____ ☐ abnormal _____

 **Listen to the following and answer the question.**

Why does the man say this: 🎧

(A) To ask a difference between normal and abnormal

(B) To contradict the woman's opinion

ORGANIZATION | Choose the best answer to complete the outline of the passage below.

Debate on the Use of Personality Pills

It can alter _____

Woman	Man
· use only for certain types of _____, only _____	· hard to decide _____ · hard to decide who is _____

(a) temporarily   (b) illness   (c) degree of severity   (d) normal or abnormal
(e) one's mind or personality

DICTATION 🎧 **Listen again and fill in the blanks.**   (P=W, S1=W, S2=M)

Professor   I think you'll agree that scientific discoveries _____ _____. A variety of pills are now _____ _____ by prescription that can _____ or personality. However, there is a strong moral dilemma over whether these pills _____. Opinions?

Student 1   Man-made substances that alter personality change a person. I believe that only certain types of illnesses, a mental disease, _____ such medicines, and _____ _____.

Student 2   I think it is hard to _____ someone should take such medicine. _____ deciding what degree of severity _____. Well, who is normal, and _____?

✔ **Check-up** for Vocabulary

Choose the correct word in the box to complete the phrases.

| scientific | available | alter | dilemma | warrant | abnormal |

1 _____ a policy

2 _____ quality

3 _____ for rent

4 _____ research

5 _____ behavior

6 get over the _____

Word Preview

☐ early graduation _____   ☐ application _____

🎧 **Listen to the following and answer the question.**

Why does the man say this: 🎧

(A) To point out to her that she is not qualified for early graduation

(B) To emphasize the improtance of the deadline

ORGANIZATION

Choose the best answer to complete the outline of the passage below.

Woman has a job opportunity
→ wants _____
→ wants to know the requirements

⇓

Requirements
(1) _____ in the top 5 %
(2) special circumstances
(3) _____
(4) _____

⇒ _____

- -

(a) an early graduation   (b) a signed agreement   (c) a grade average   (d) submit an application
(e) meet all deadlines

DICTATION 🎧 **Listen again and fill in the blanks.** (S=W, C=M)

Student	Hi. _____ about the possibility of graduating early. I have a job opportunity that _____ but I need to graduate first.
Counselor	Well, it's not common, but some students can graduate early. _____ a grade average in the top five percent, special circumstances, and _____ from all of your lecturers.
Student	My grades _____ this term, and I'm very _____ my ambitions.
Counselor	That's all _____, but... I see that _____ two deadlines this semester. If you want to graduate early, you _____ in the future.
Student	Okay. I will.
Counselor	You should submit your application for early graduation to student administration, only when you keep the rest of the deadlines.

✓ **Check-up** **for Vocabulary**

Choose the correct word in the box to complete the phrases.

graduate	sign	achieve	deadline	submit	application

1 _____ our names

2 _____ a resume

3 _____ success

4 meet the _____

5 _____ from Oxford

6 fill out a(n) _____

■ Exercise 1

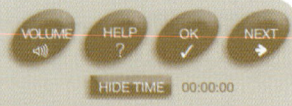

TOEFL Listening

VOLUME   HELP   OK   NEXT
                    ?   ✓

HIDE TIME   00:00:00

🎧 **Listen to a lecture in an ancient history class then answer the questions.**

1 **Why does the professor mention a soul of a person?**
   (A) To emphasize that Egyptians believe in the future existence
   (B) To give an example of a well-made mummies
   (C) To provide a reason why Egyptians made mummies
   (D) To explain the difficulties of preserving the body with a soul

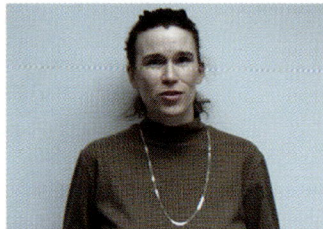

2 **Which of the following is NOT the process of making a mummy?**
   (A) Putting the heart in a coffin.
   (B) Covering the body with cloth.
   (C) Emptying the body's skull.
   (D) Filling the body with sawdust.

* embalming fluid 방부제

🎧 **Listen again and fill in the blanks. You may use your notes to help you answer the questions.**

Mummy in Egypt
· Philosophy _____ will live on _____
· Process   1. take out _____
             2. stuff the _____
             3. fill the body with embalming fluid
             4. _____ in cloth
             5. place it _____

Exercise 2

TOEFL Listening

VOLUME ◁)) | HELP ? | OK ✓ | NEXT →

HIDE TIME 00:00:00

🎧 **Listen to a talk in a computer class then answer the questions.**

1 **Why does the professor mention Portuguese hackers?**

(A) To give a name of a famous hacker in Europe

(B) To exemplify real hackers and what they do

(C) To explain the most common way to get into a system

(D) To show how hacking can damage a system

2 **According to the professor, what does hacking mean?**

(A) Being a very young computer programmer.

(B) Changing a computer system without permission from the government.

(C) Being very good at entering computer systems.

(D) Entering computer systems without permission.

CHAPTER 6

🎧 **Listen again and fill in the blanks. You may use your notes to help you answer the questions.**

Hacking is – access to a computer system _____

e.g. Portuguese Hackers

→ _____

→ for 3 hours

→ do not _____ any information

 **Exercise 3**

TOEFL Listening

VOLUME   HELP   OK   NEXT
   ?

HIDE TIME   00:00:00

🎧 **Listen to a discussion in a social studies class then answer the questions.**

1 **Why does the professor say this:** 🎧
   (A) To encourage students to participate in the class
   (B) To ask if the students have done their assignment
   (C) To imply that most initial thoughts of people are wrong
   (D) To give a general assumption of fox hunting

2 **Why does the woman mention fox hunting season?**
   (A) To point out that people cannot hunt all year
   (B) To point out that fox hunting is a very cruel sport
   (C) To point out that people even hunt pregnant or nursing foxes
   (D) To point out that it is too easy to kill a pregnant fox

🎧 **Listen again and fill in the blanks. You may use your notes to help you answer the questions.**

Fox Hunting
 ─ Student 1   "Positive"
                  · The fox is _____ .
                     ∴ need to be controlled
                  · Can control _____ livestock or other
 ─ Student 2   "Negative"
                  · Hunters do not keep _____
                     ∴ _____ are killed

128

Exercise 4

TOEFL Listening   VOLUME   HELP ?   OK ✓   NEXT →

HIDE TIME   00:00:00

🎧 **Listen to a conversation between two students then answer the questions.**

1 Why does the woman say this: 🎧

(A) To complain about the man's behavior

(B) To persuade that the man should go

(C) To protect the professor from getting hurt

(D) To help the man do well in college

2 What will the man probably do next?

(A) Do some painting.

(B) Go shopping.

(C) Call his friend.

(D) Call the professor.

🎧 **Listen again and fill in the blanks. You may use your notes to help you answer the questions.**

Field trip

    · Date   – _____

    · Problem   – _____

                 – The professor _____ above all else

   ⇒ Woman's Suggestion : _____ and cancel the appointment

                              : _____

Dictation for Exercise

Exercise 1

🎧 **Listen and fill in the blanks.**   (P=W)

Professor A mummy is ① _____. Egyptians believed that every

person had a soul that ② _____ and if the person's

body was destroyed, the spirit might not be able to survive. To properly

preserve the body ③ _____, it would have to be

mummified. The Egyptian body preservation process was a complicated

procedure ④ _____ priests. They took out the brain and most

of the internal organs, ⑤ _____ sawdust or linen

pads. Then they filled the body with an embalming fluid. Finally, they

⑥ _____ in cloth and ⑦ _____ in a coffin that

was shaped like a human. Egyptians that were mummified were normally

the most important in society, so they had many of their riches or treasures

⑧ _____.

|구문해설| **mummy** 미라 **afterlife** 사후, 내세 **procedure** 절차, 진행 **priest** 성직자 **internal organs** 내장 **stuff ~ with...**
~을 …로 채우다 **sawdust** 톱밥 **coffin** 관

✔ **Check-up** for Expression

Complete the sentences using given words or phrases.

be able to	performed by	complicated procedures

1 The work was _____ a robot.

2 We would _____ make a more profit.

3 We need to simplify the _____ to meet the deadline.

130

Exercise 2

🎧 **Listen and fill in the blanks.** (P=M, S=W)

Professor   Hacking is when a person ① _____ a computer system without authorization. Some of the major computer hacking that ② _____ _____ has been done by teenagers. For example, some Portuguese hackers once ③ _____ on the web page of the Indonesian government, focusing on that country's continued oppression of East Timor. The attack was ④ _____ at the web site of the Department of Foreign Affairs in the Republic of Indonesia. What do you think that the hackers did?

Student   Did they ⑤ _____ the system and ⑥ _____?

Professor   No. Real hackers do not delete or destroy any information on the system ⑦ _____. Hackers do what they do because they love ⑧ _____ _____ getting into a system that is ⑨ _____. The Portuguese hackers did not delete or change anything. They said, 'We just ⑩ _____.'

|구문해설| **hacking** 해킹   **gain access to ~** ~에 접근[출입]하다   **without authorization** 허가 없이   **launch an attack** 공격을 개시하다   **mess up** ~을 엉망으로 만들다, ~에 충격을 주다

✔ Check-up for Expression

Complete the sentences using given words or phrases.

gain access to	launch an attack	mess up

1   The unexpected effect _____ the project.

2   Enter the user name and password to _____ the network resource.

3   The organization _____ against the government.

CHAPTER 6

Dictation for Exercise

Exercise 3

🎧 **Listen and fill in the blanks.**

(P=M, S1=M, S2=W)

Professor In Britain, amongst certain people, fox hunting is a popular sport. Today we're going to discuss ① _____ fox hunting. ② _____ _____. about this?

Student 1 The fox is a pest and its population ③ _____. Any concerned farmers would agree with this. Responsible fox management includes maintaining a healthy fox population ④ _____ livestock or other wildlife.

Student 2 But the official fox hunting season ⑤ _____ November to April; yet fox cubs are usually born in March, which means that ⑥ _____ _____ are hunted and killed. Is this right?

Student 1 Foxes cause significant lamb, piglet, and poultry losses. Fox hunting is the most natural method of management. ⑦ _____ the old, sick, and injured foxes. ⑧ _____ fox hunting they would overpopulate and would eventually have to be ⑨ _____, or gassed.

|구문해설| **initial** 초기의, 처음의 **threaten** 위협[협박]하다 **livestock** 가축(류) **cub** 어린 짐승, 짐승 새끼 **nursing** 양육 받는, 젖먹이의 **poultry** 가금(류) **overpopulate** 과밀화시키다, 인구 과잉으로 하다

✔ **Check-up** for Expression

Complete the sentences using given words or phrases.

method of	agree with	be going to

1 His hypothesis does not _____ the facts.

2 They _____ spend a lot of time to discuss the issue.

3 The college will adopt a new _____ teaching.

Exercise 4

🎧 **Listen and fill in the blanks.**

(S1=M, S2=W)

Student 1 Oh, I ① _____ a field trip this weekend. I have so many things to do.

Student 2 Yeah, me too. I need to do some shopping. But I guess ② _____ next week. I'll see you there.

Student 1 Actually, I'm thinking of ③ _____. I promised to help my friend do some painting. I don't think ④ _____ if I'm not there.

Student 2 Really? You know… the professor strongly values attendance ⑤ _____.

Student 1 That's true! *(Sigh…)*

Student 2 I guess your friend will understand if you can't help her.

Student 1 Yeah, maybe. ⑥ _____.

Student 2 Sounds like ⑦ _____. See you on the weekend then.

Student 1 Okay, see you. And thanks for the good advice.

Student 2 Anytime.

|구문해설| **field trip** (학생의) 실지 견학, 야외 연구 여행   **give ~ a miss** 빼먹다, 결석하다

✔ Check-up for Expression

Complete the sentences using given words or phrases.

field trip	not matter if	attendance

1 It _____ you did it on purpose or not.

2 I don't think the _____ educational.

3 The professor was upset that student _____ was very low.

Vocabulary Review

Write the meanings of the words or phrases in the blanks.

1 pilot _____

2 questionnaire _____

3 conduct _____

4 common _____

5 available _____

6 dilemma _____

7 fix _____

8 sign _____

9 submit _____

10 resource _____

11 prescription _____

12 correct _____

13 species _____

14 warrant _____

15 mummy _____

16 initial _____

17 experiment _____

18 graduate _____

19 alter _____

20 abnormal _____

21 instruction _____

22 organism _____

23 accidentally _____

24 coffin _____

25 hacking _____

26 priest _____

27 nursing _____

28 poultry _____

29 procedure _____

30 afterlife _____

31 threaten _____

32 livestock _____

33 overpopulate _____

34 internal organs _____

35 field trip _____

36 stuff ~ with... _____

37 gain access to ~ _____

38 give ~ a miss _____

39 launch an attack _____

40 mess up _____

FINAL TEST

Listing Comprehension Section Directions

This section measures your ability to understand conversations and lectures in English. You will hear each conversation or lecture only one time. After each conversation or lecture, you will answer some questions about it. The questions typically ask about the main idea and supporting details. Some questions ask about a speaker's purpose or attitude. Answer the questions based on what is stated or implied by the speakers.

You may take notes while you listen. You may use your notes to help you answer the questions. Your notes will not be scored. If you need to change the volume while you listen, click on the **Volume** icon at the top of the screen. In some questions, you will see this icon: 🎧 This means that you will hear, but not see part of the question.

Some of the questions have special directions. These directions appear in a gray box on the screen. Most questions are worth one point. If a question is worth more than one point, it will have special directions that indicate how many points you can receive. You must answer each question. After you answer, click on **Next**. Then click on **OK** to confirm your answer and go on to the next question. After you click on **OK**, you cannot return to previous questions.

You will have 20 minutes to answer the questions in this section. A clock at the top of the screen will show you how much time is remaining. The clock will not count down while you are listening to test material.

Final Test 1

🎧 **Listen to a lecture in a literature class then answer the questions.**

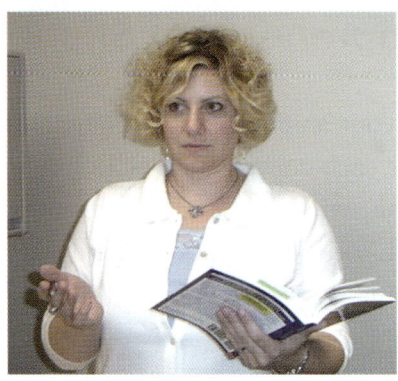

1 What is the lecture mainly about?

    Ⓐ A very famous poet

    Ⓑ The role of the reader

    Ⓒ The role of the listener

    Ⓓ A particular form of poetry

2 What does the professor say about Robert Browning?

    Ⓐ He invented modern poetry called dramatic monologue.

    Ⓑ He was also a great writer of dramas.

    Ⓒ He was excellent at reciting this style of poetry.

    Ⓓ He had had a great influence on modern poetry.

3 According to the professor, which of the following is NOT a characteristic of Robert Browning's monologues?

    Ⓐ The reader plays the role of a silent listener.

    Ⓑ The reader determines the wider story.

    Ⓒ The reader argues with the speaker in public.

    Ⓓ The reader and the speaker are involved.

4 How does the professor explain dramatic monologue?

    Ⓐ By showing how to write a dramatic monologue

    Ⓑ By analyzing Browning's writing style

    Ⓒ By giving examples of pieces of work

    Ⓓ By comparing it with modern poetry

Final Test 2

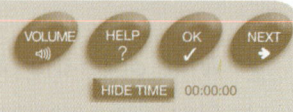
🎧 **Listen to a conversation between a student and an administrator then answer the questions.**

1 Why does the woman go to see the man?

Ⓐ To pay for her lunch

Ⓑ To ask him out for dinner

Ⓒ To ask how meals work this term

Ⓓ To complain about the school meal plan

2 **According to the conversation, which of the following is true? Choose TWO answers.**

   Ⓐ Option one includes a dessert but option three doesn't.

   Ⓑ Option two offers a dessert and a starter.

   Ⓒ Option one includes a dessert but option two doesn't.

   Ⓓ Option three includes the main meal but not a starter or dessert.

3 **Listen to part of the conversation again.** 🎧

   What does the man mean when he says this: 🎧

   Ⓐ The food has not been very good.

   Ⓑ The meal is not big enough for students.

   Ⓒ Students have paied too much for the meal.

   Ⓓ The new plan is designed to meet each student's capacity for food.

4 **What will the woman probably do next?**

   Ⓐ Go to the cafeteria.

   Ⓑ Fill in the form.

   Ⓒ Choose an option.

   Ⓓ Pay for the meal.

Final Test 3

🎧 **Listen to a lecture in an anthropology class then answer the questions.**

* tepee (북미 원주민의) 원뿔형 천막집

1 **What is the lecture mainly about?**

   Ⓐ How fierce the Blackfoot Indians were
   Ⓑ How the Blackfoot Indians hunted
   Ⓒ The dangers caused by Blackfoot Indians
   Ⓓ The life of the Blackfoot Indians

2 What are two main reasons that the Blackfoot Indian population declined? Choose TWO answers.

    Ⓐ Because they got very sick.

    Ⓑ Because the climate suddenly changed.

    Ⓒ Because the buffalo decreased.

    Ⓓ Because they lived in teepees.

3 According to the professor, for what did the Indians use buffalo? Choose THREE answers.

    Ⓐ To make useful equipment.

    Ⓑ To make things to wear.

    Ⓒ To make weapons.

    Ⓓ To make use of it as money.

4 According to the professor, which of the following is true about Blackfoot Indians?

    Ⓐ Men had great skills at building the shelters.

    Ⓑ Women were responsible for making weapons or tools.

    Ⓒ They didn't suffer from disease.

    Ⓓ They lived mainly on herbs or fish.

Final Test 4

🎧 **Listen to a talk in psychology class then answer the questions.**

1 **What is the talk mainly about?**

  Ⓐ Fears that make no sense

  Ⓑ Usual and unusual fears

  Ⓒ Three psychological problems

  Ⓓ Phobias and their causes

2 Indicate the following and click on the correct box for each phrase.

	Simple phobia	Social phobia	Agora- phobia
Fear of things such as frogs or spiders			
Fear of being in large or busy places			
An extreme fear of specific objects			
Feeling embarrassed when with people			
Being afraid of a panic attack			
Fear of speaking in front of a crowd			

3 Why does the professor mention hippopotomonstrosesquippedaliophobia?

(A) To show her skill at saying long words

(B) To check that the students are listening

(C) To make the talk humorous and memorable

(D) To give an example of unusual phobias

4 Listen to part of the talk again. 🎧

What does the professor imply when she says this: 🎧

(A) Agoraphobia has no specific target to fear.

(B) Agoraphobia is easily explained.

(C) Agoraphobia is not a fear at all.

(D) Agoraphobia has no special traits to distinguish it from other phobias.

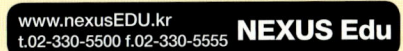

수준별 맞춤

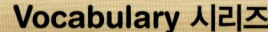

Vocabulary 시리즈

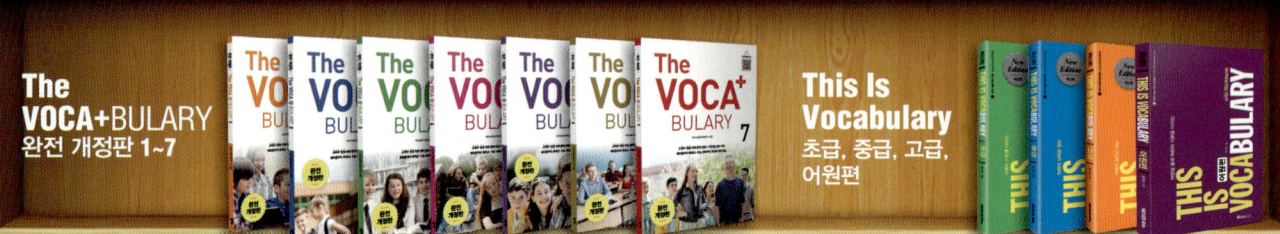

The VOCA+BULARY
완전 개정판 1~7

This Is Vocabulary
초급, 중급, 고급, 어원편

Grammar 시리즈

Grammar 공감
Level 1~3

도전 만점 중등 내신 서술형 1~4

Grammar Bridge
Level 1~3
개정판

초등필수 영문법+쓰기 1, 2

The Grammar with Workbook
starter
Level 1~3

OK Grammar
Level 1~4

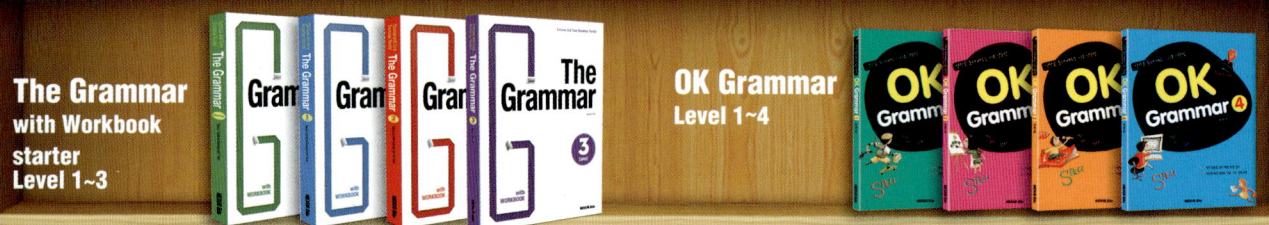

After School Grammar
Level 1~3

This Is Grammar
초급 1·2
중급 1·2
고급 1·2

성공적인 학습을 위한 단계별 전략!
Development & Progress for Completion

NEXUS
TOEFL®
iBT

정답 및 해설

Listening

Starter

NEXUS Edu

CHAPTER 01
MAIN IDEA

Sample

생물학 수업의 강의를 듣고 물음에 답하시오.

교수 항생물질은 우리 사회에서 중요한 역할을 합니다. 항생물질은 살아 있는 박테리아가 증식하지 못하게 하거나, 이들을 죽입니다. 일부 항생물질은 균류나 곰팡이와 같은 살아 있는 유기체로부터 자연적으로 생성되기도 하지만 또 어떤 것들은 일부 혹은 전체가 인공물질이기도 합니다. 그러니까 과학자들에 의해 합성된 것이죠. 아마도 페니실린이 자연적 혹은 인공적 형태 둘 다를 아우르는 가장 유명한 항생물질일 겁니다. 페니실린의 발견은 인류의 가장 위대한 업적 중의 하나이죠. 페니실린은 수백만 명의 생명을 구했습니다. 항생물질을 통해 의학계에 종사하는 사람들은 많은 전염병을 효과적으로 치료할 수 있었고, 많은 전염병이 더 이상 사람의 생명을 위협하지 않게 만들었습니다.

강의의 주된 내용은 무엇인가?
(A) 항생물질의 가치
(B) 페니실린이라 불리는 특별한 종류의 약
(C) 항생물질의 기원
(D) 항생물질의 부작용

정답 (A)

해설 주제를 묻는 문제의 경우, 전반적인 내용을 전부 이해하기에 앞서 핵심 시그널이 될 부분을 파악해 두는 것이 중요하다. 강의의 첫 부분에서 교수는 Antibiotics play a major role in our society.라고 언급함으로써 앞으로 항생물질의 중요성에 대해 살펴볼 것임을 암시했다.

Skill Check-up

다음을 듣고 물음에 답하시오.

🎧 스크립트

S1 Can you help me?
S2 What's wrong?
S1 This essay, I have no idea where to start.
S2 It's simple, just answer the question!
S1 But look! It isn't a question.
S2 Hmmm… You're right, it's a statement. Do you know what I do when they give me a statement not a question?
S1 No, what?
S2 I turn it into a question by asking questions

about everything in the statement and…
S1 Wait, I get it! The questions that I ask tell me what I need to know!
S2 Yes! When you have questions you know what research you have to do to get the answers.
S1 Whew! Thanks! Now I know how to start working on this essay.

학생1 나 좀 도와줄 수 있니?
학생2 무슨 일이니?
학생1 이 보고서 말이야. 어디서부터 시작해야 할지 도통 모르겠어.
학생2 간단해. 그냥 질문에 답하면 되잖아.
학생1 하지만 이것 좀 봐. 이건 질문이 아니야.
학생2 음, 그렇네. 이건 서술문이구나. 질문이 아닌 서술문이 주어지는 경우에 난 어떻게 하는지 아니?
학생1 아니 몰라. 어떻게 하는데?
학생2 서술문에 있는 모든 내용에 대해 물어보면서 그 서술문을 질문으로 바꿔보는 거지. 그러면…
학생1 잠깐, 무슨 말인지 알겠어! 내가 묻는 질문들이 바로 내가 알아야 할 것들이란 거구나!
학생2 그래. (자신에게) 질문을 해보면 거기에 답하기 위해 어떤 연구를 해야 하는지 알게 되는 거야.
학생1 휴! 고마워. 이제 보고서를 어떻게 시작해야 할지 알겠어.

여자가 남자를 찾아간 이유는 무엇인가?
(A) 보고서 작성에 대해 조언을 구하려고
(B) 보고서에 관한 정보를 어디서 찾을 수 있는지 물어보려고

정답 (A)

해설 여학생은 어떻게 보고서를 작성해야 하는지 전혀 감을 잡지 못하겠다고 말하며 남학생에게 도움을 구하고 있다.

Word Preview

☐ **statement** (주제의) 제시, 진술문　☐ **research** 연구, 탐구

ORGANIZATION

(c) → (b) → (a)

(※ 정답은 '위에서 아래로', '왼쪽에서 오른쪽으로' 순서대로 표기함. 이하동일)

Check-up for Vocabulary

1. wok on the new project 새 프로젝트 일을 하다
2. market research 시장 조사
3. turn it into English (~을) 영어로 바꾸다
4. make a statement 진술하다

Skill Check-up 2

다음을 듣고 물음에 답하시오.

🎧 스크립트

> P Today I'd like to focus on the effects of advertising on our perception of the female. One of these effects could be women's desire of being perfect size. This is because how women are portrayed in most ads. But beauty is most definitely in the eye of the beholder! In some centuries physically ideal women were almost fat not thin. We celebrate thinness as the ideal image of beauty, but in the past it indicated unhealthiness: thin people equaled hungry, sick people. Later, when you write your essays, I will expect you to demonstrate this concept; that beauty is not an absolute truth, but a media construct: in other words an idea not a fact.

교수 오늘은 여성에 대한 우리의 인식에 광고가 미치는 영향을 중점적으로 다루려 합니다. 그 중 하나는 완벽한 몸매에 대한 여성들의 욕망이라 할 수 있을 겁니다. 이것은 대부분의 광고에 나타나는 여성의 이미지 때문에 그런 것입니다. 하지만 '미'라는 것은 절대적으로 보는 사람의 눈에 따라 다르기 마련입니다. 수 세기 동안 여성의 이상적인 신체는 마른 것이 아니라 거의 뚱뚱할 정도의 것이었습니다. 우리는 마른 신체를 미의 이상적인 이미지로 찬미하지만, 과거에 말랐다는 것은 건강하지 못한 것으로 여겨졌습니다. 마른 사람은 굶주리거나 병약한 사람과 동일했습니다. 나중에 여러분이 과제를 쓸 경우에는 이같은 개념에 대해 설명하시기 바랍니다. 미란 절대적인 진리가 아니라 미디어가 만들어낸 것이라는 점, 다시 말해서 진실이 아닌 (일반적인) 관념이라는 것에 대해서 말입니다.

강의는 주로 무엇에 관한 것이겠는가?
(A) 완벽한 여성상에 대해 광고가 미치는 영향
(B) 건강한 여성상에 대해 광고가 미치는 영향

정답 (A)

해설 강의 첫 부분(Today I'd like to focus on ~)을 보면 여성의 완벽함에 대한 사람들의 인식에 광고가 미치는 영향이 강의 주제임을 알 수 있다.

Word Preview

☐ perception 인지, 인식　　☐ beholder 보는 사람, 구경꾼
☐ equal ~와 같다　　☐ concept 개념, 발상

ORGANIZATION
(d) → (a) → (b) → (c)

Check-up for Vocabulary
1. celebrate Christmas 크리스마스를 축하하다
2. an ideal world 이상적인 세계
3. advertise a house for sale 집을 팔려고 광고하다
4. indicate a place on the street 거리의 한 곳을 지적하다
5. demonstrate how to use the machine
   기계 사용 방법을 설명하다
6. a new concept of the universe 우주에 대한 새로운 개념

Skill Check-up 3

다음을 듣고 물음에 답하시오.

🎧 스크립트

> P Eating disorders are becoming more common. Let's begin with the following kinds; anorexia nervosa, anorexia athletica, bulimia, and binge eating. Can any of you define these conditions for me?
> S Anorexia nervosa is a fear of eating; anorexia athletica is where athletes avoid food and lose too much weight; bulimia is eating then vomiting to empty the stomach; and binge eating is consuming extremely large amounts of food in a single meal.
> P Correct! Well done! People with these disorders can eventually die. So it is vital that we recognize warning signs and detect eating problems early, so that people can return to a normal life as quickly as possible. Today we will examine some of the major reasons for this happening. We will consider biological, mental, and social causes.

교수 음식물 섭취 장애(섭식 장애) 가 더욱 흔하게 발생하고 있습니다. 다음 종류의 섭식장애에 관해 알아보죠. 거식증, 식욕 감퇴, 과식증, 대식증에 대해서요. 이런 증상에 대해 정의를 내려볼 사람이 있나요?
학생 거식증은 먹는 것을 두려워하는 증상입니다. 식욕 감퇴는 운동선수들이 음식을 기피해서 너무나 많은 체중이 빠지는 증상입니다. 과식증은 음식을 먹고 나서 위장을 비우기 위해 토하는 증상이고, 대식증은 한 번의 식사에 지나치게 많은 양의 음식을 먹는 것이죠.
교수 맞습니다. 훌륭하군요. 이런 장애를 가진 사람들은 결국 사망할 가능성까지 있습니다. 그렇기 때문에 경고 신호를 알아

차리고 초기에 이런 문제를 감지하는 것이 대단히 중요합니다. 그래야 사람들이 가능한 한 빨리 정상적인 생활로 돌아올 수 있습니다. 오늘 우리는 이러한 장애가 발생하는 몇 가지 주요 원인을 살펴보겠습니다. 즉 생물학적, 정신적, 사회적 원인들에 대해 알아보겠습니다.

주로 어떤 내용의 강의가 이어지겠는가?
(A) 음식물 섭취 장애의 여러 가지 형태
(B) 음식물 섭취 장애의 여러 가지 원인

정답 (B)

해설 첫부분에서 교수는 강의에서 사용할 여러 용어에 대해 언급하였고, 강의에서 다룰 주제는 마지막 부분(Today we will examine some of the major reasons ~)에서 언급하고 있다.

Word Preview

- ☐ **anorexia** 식욕 감퇴
- ☐ **anorexia nervosa** 거식증
- ☐ **anorexia athletica** 식욕 감퇴
- ☐ **bulimia** 과식증, 폭식증
- ☐ **bnge eating** 대식증

ORGANIZATION

(b) → (e) → (c) → (d) → (a)

Check-up for Vocabulary

1. empty the trash 쓰레기통을 비우다
2. detect crimes 죄를 잡아내다
3. mental disorder 정신적 장애
4. warn of danger 위험을 경고하다
5. consume gas 가스를 소비하다
6. a vital wound 치명상

Skill Check-up **4**

다음을 듣고 물음에 답하시오.

🎧 스크립트

> P Traditional art plays a major part in the day to day life of African tribal society. Together we'll explore the three basic themes of African art. The first is the dualism between bush and village; nature verses civilization. Wearing special masks or headdresses, African tribes express those ideas. The second is the relationships between the sexes. African tribes use art to deal with the problems and issues between man and woman relationships. The third theme is the effort to control natural or supernatural power. They often use masks in ceremonies to please and honor the forces that affect the day to day life of the tribe.

교수 아프리카 부족 사회의 일상생활에서 전통 예술은 중요한 역할을 담당합니다. 다같이 아프리카 예술의 세 가지 기본 주제에 대해 살펴보겠습니다. 첫 번째는 아프리카의 오지와 촌락 간의 이원성, 즉 자연 대 문명입니다. 아프리카 부족들은 특이한 가면이나 머리 장식물을 사용해서 이런 개념을 표현합니다. 두 번째는 남성과 여성 간의 관계입니다. 아프리카 부족들은 남녀 관계에서 발생하는 문제나 사건들을 다루는 데 이 (전통) 예술을 사용하지요. 세 번째 주제는 자연적 혹은 초자연적 힘을 통제하려는 노력입니다. 이들은 자기 부족들의 일상 생활에 영향을 미치는 자연의 힘을 숭배하고 찬미하는 의식에서 종종 가면을 사용합니다.

강의의 주된 내용은 무엇인가?
(A) 전통적인 아프리카 예술의 역할
(B) 전통적인 아프리카 예술의 주제

정답 (B)

해설 Together we'll explore ~와 같은 시그널에 유념하자. 아프리카 예술의 3가지 기본 주제에 관해 살펴보겠다고 했다.

Word Preview

- ☐ **tribal** 부족의
- ☐ **bush** (아프리카) 미개지, 관목 숲
- ☐ **civilization** 문명
- ☐ **headdress** 머리 장식물
- ☐ **supernatural** 초자연의, 불가사의한

ORGANIZATION

(a) → (d) → (c) → (b)

Check-up for Vocabulary

1. expore remote islands 멀리 떨어진 섬을 탐험하다
2. Western civilization 서구 문명
3. deal with the situation 상황에 대처하다
4. a parent-child relationship 부모 자식 관계
5. the theme of a music 음악의 주제
6. traditional dress or food 전통 의상이나 (전통) 음식

Exercise

■ Exercise 1

음악 수업의 토론을 듣고 물음에 답하시오.

🎧 스크립트

> P Punk rock was originally created to express feelings about corrupt governments and other social issues. Modern punk rock seems to have become more about entertainment and less about protest.
> S1 Well... that makes sense because modern punk rock lyrics are more about relationships and life and sometimes the songs and groups

are now even funny. It's like we have two forms of punk rock; modern and primitive.

S2 I don't agree. I think that modern punk rock isn't really punk rock at all, it's something different: it's no longer true to its origins. Groups became commerical. They became money focused!

P Well, yes, some people have suggested that they sold out, however, didn't it have to evolve to survive? I'd suggest that it had to become more commercial to find a larger audience.

교수 펑크 록은 원래 부패한 정부와 기타 사회문제에 대한 감정을 표현하기 위해 만들어진 것이었습니다. (그러나) 현대의 펑크 록은 점점 더 흥미위주로 바뀌고 보다 덜 저항적인 것 같습니다.

학생1 음... 그런 것 같아요. 현대 펑크 록은 (인간) 관계와 삶에 대해 더욱 많이 노래하고 있지요. 때때로 이런 노래나 록 그룹은 이제 재미나기까지 합니다. 마치 우리에게는 현대와 원시라는 두 가지 형태의 펑크 록이 존재하는 것 같습니다.

학생2 제 생각은 다릅니다. 현대의 펑크 록이라는 것은 진정한 의미에서 전혀 펑크 록이 아니라고 생각합니다. 뭔가 다른 음악이에요. 그룹은 상업화되었고, 돈에 초점을 맞추고 있습니다.

교수 음, 그렇죠. 어떤 사람들은 그들이 변질되었다고 주장하기도 합니다. 하지만 그들도 살아남기 위해서는 변해야만 하지 않았을까요? 보다 많은 청중을 찾기 위해 좀더 상업적으로 변해야만 했다는 것이 제 생각입니다.

1 **토론의 주된 내용은 무엇인가?**
(A) 펑크 록이 정부에 미친 영향
(B) 펑크 록의 변화
(C) 펑크 록의 부정적 영향
(D) 펑크 록의 상업주의

정답 (B)

해설 기존의 펑크 록과 현대의 펑크 록의 차이, 그리고 그러한 변화가 일어나게 된 원인에 대해 토론한다.

2 **교수의 말에 따르면, 원래의 펑크 록은 어떤 음악인가?**
(A) 부패한 정부에 저항하는 매우 감성적인 음악
(B) 사람들을 기쁘게 해주는 오락성 음악
(C) 오락성에 저항하는 강렬한 음악
(D) 변화의 필요성을 노래하는 감성적 음악

정답 (A)

해설 첫 부분에서 교수가 말하기를 펑크 록의 원래 목적은 부패한 정부와 기타 사회문제에 대한 감정을 표현하는 것이라고 했다.

ORGANIZATION

corrupt governments / social issues, entertainment / protest, relationships / life

■ Exercise 2

의학 수업의 대화를 듣고 물음에 답하시오.

🎧 스크립트

P Many Americans are turning to acupuncture to deal with health issues. Acupuncture can be defined as being healed by inserting needles into specific points of the body.

S Why do they think that's better than modern drugs?

P Good question! The idea is drugs only treat the symptoms but acupuncture cures the cause.

S How?

P Well, this is the idea that we need an unobstructed flow of 'Qi' to be healthy. 'Qi' is believed to be the basic energy that constitutes everything that exists. In our bodies there are two opposing forces, 'yin' (water) and 'yang' (fire). If they are out of balance this blocks the flow of 'Qi' through our bodies causing illness. Sticking needles in specific parts of the body restores balance, 'Qi' flows again, and good health is restored.

교수 많은 미국인들이 건강 문제와 관련해 침술에 의지하고 있습니다. 침술은 신체의 특정 부위에 바늘을 꽂아 질병을 치유하는 것으로 정의될 수 있습니다.

학생 사람들이 현대 의학보다 침술이 낫다고 생각하는 이유는 무엇입니까?

교수 좋은 질문이군요. 말하자면 그건, 약은 증상만을 치료하지만 침술은 (병의) 원인을 치유한다고 생각하는 데서 나옵니다.

학생 어떻게요?

교수 아, 이런 이치입니다. 건강을 유지하려면 '기'의 흐름이 막히지 말아야 합니다. '기'란 존재하는 모든 것을 구성하는 기본적인 에너지라고 여겨지는 것인데요. 우리의 신체에는 물을 상징하는 '음'과 불을 상징하는 '양'의 두 가지 반대되는 힘이 존재합니다. 이 두 가지 힘이 균형을 잃게 되면 신체를 통과하는 '기'의 흐름을 막게 되어 병이 생깁니다. 특정 신체 부위에 바늘을 꽂음으로써 이 균형을 회복하면 '기'가 다시 원활하게 흘러 건강이 회복되는 것이죠.

1 강의의 주된 내용은 무엇인가?

(A) 원활한 기(흐름)의 중요성
(B) 미국인이 선호하는 것
(C) 침술이 효력을 발휘하는 방식
(D) 의약이 효력이 없는 이유

정답 (C)

해설 교수는 미국인들이 침술에 의존하게 된 이유를 설명하면서 침술의 원리와 효력에 대해 설명하고 있다.

2 교수에 따르면, 미국인들이 침술을 현대 의약보다 낫다고 생각하는 이유는 무엇인가?

(A) 침술은 증상을 완화시킨다.
(B) 침술은 건강을 증진시킨다.
(C) 침술의 효과가 더 빠르다.
(D) 침술은 병의 원인을 치유한다.

정답 (D)

해설 현대의 의약은 병의 증상만을 치료하지만 침술은 병의 원인을 없앤다고 생각하기 때문이다.

ORGANIZATION

inserting needles,
water and fire,
cures the causes

■ Exercise 3

경제 수업의 강의를 듣고 물음에 답하시오.

🎧 스크립트

P Today we will look at planning. There is a saying 'Fail to plan, plan to fail!' Yes, I can see some of you want to say that nobody plans to fail. However, many businesses do fail because they don't plan. In a business plan there are three key factors: determining if a market need exists, establishing an operating budget, and estimating how long it will take to make a profit. Many great products have failed because there was no market need. It does not matter that a product is great. What matters is enough people want to buy that product. Many companies go bankrupt because they have no budget and overspend. It is also unwise to keep pouring money into a business hoping it will eventually become successful. We have to know when to give up. Planning does not guarantee success but failing to plan can guarantee failure.

교수 오늘은 계획 수립에 대해 살펴보겠습니다. '계획하지 않는 것은 실패를 계획하는 것이다.'라는 말이 있죠. 네, 여러분 중에 몇 명은 실패를 계획하는 사람이 어디 있냐고 할 겁니다. 그러나 계획을 제대로 세우지 못해서 많은 사업체들이 실패를 하고 있습니다. 사업 계획에는 세 가지 주요 요소가 있습니다. 시장 수요가 존재하는지를 확정하는 것, 운영할 자금을 형성하는 것, 그리고 수익을 거두는 데 걸리는 시간을 추정하는 것 등입니다. 훌륭한 제품임에도 시장 수요가 없다는 이유로 실패하는 제품들이 많이 있습니다. 제품이 훌륭한지는 문제되지 않습니다. 중요한 것은 충분한 수요의 사람들이 그 제품을 사고 싶어하는지 입니다. 다수의 회사들은 자금이 없거나 지출을 낭비해서 파산 지경에 이릅니다. 종국에 가서는 성공하리라 희망하면서 사업에 돈을 퍼붓는 것 또한 현명하지 못합니다. 포기할 때가 언제인지도 알아야 합니다. 계획을 수립한다고 해서 성공이 보장되지는 않지만 계획을 세우지 않는다는 것은 실패를 확정짓는 것이 분명합니다.

1 강의의 주된 내용은 무엇인가?

(A) 사업을 시작하는 방법
(B) 실패를 피하고 성공하는 방법
(C) 사업 계획의 중요성
(D) 운용 예산의 중요성

정답 (C)

해설 교수는 격언을 사용해서 사업계획 수립의 중요성을 부각시킨 후, 사업 계획의 중요한 세 가지 요소를 짚어가며 설명하고 있다. 사업의 실패나 성공 요인에 대한 구체적인 설명을 하는 것이 아니므로 (B)는 답이 될 수 없다.

2 교수에 따르면, 다음 중 (사업 계획의) 주요 요소가 아닌 것은?

(A) 사람들이 제품을 필요로 하는지 알아내는 것
(B) 운영 자금을 조달하는 것
(C) 수익 창출 시기를 추정하는 것
(D) 훌륭한 제품을 공급하는 것

정답 (D)

해설 훌륭한 제품의 공급은 주요 요소로 언급되지 않았다. 오히려 아무리 제품이 훌륭하더라도 제품에 대한 수요가 없으면 실패한다고 경고하고 있다.

ORGANIZATION

Business Planning,
a market need exists,
an operating budget,
make a profit

■ Exercise 4

학생과 상담자와의 대화를 듣고 물음에 답하시오.

🎧 스크립트

S Excuse me! Can you help me?
C Certainly sir! What do you need?

S I'm not happy with my dorm room, I want to move.

C Oh! I'm sorry to hear that. What's the problem?

S I can't study because my roommate is too noisy. I'd like to know if there is a single dorm available.

C Well, let's see! Hmmm… just as I thought, there are none left.

S Well, what can I do? I'll go mad if I have to keep living with this guy.

C You could try a different roommate. I have a list here of students looking for someone to share their dorm. Or you could try our off campus accommodation list.

S Okay, can I have a copy of both lists? I'll try them both.

C Sure, you can have these. Good luck!

학생 실례합니다. 저 좀 도와주시겠어요?
상담자 물론이죠! 무슨 일이신가요?
학생 기숙사가 맘에 안 들어서 옮기고 싶어요.
상담자 이런, 안타깝군요. 무슨 문제인가요?
학생 룸메이트가 너무 시끄러워서 공부를 할 수가 없어요. 1인실이 있는지 알고 싶습니다.
상담자 음, 한번 볼게요. 흠… 예상했던 대로 비어있는 방이 하나도 없군요.
학생 그럼, 어떻게 하죠? 이 친구와 계속 함께 살면 정말 미쳐버리고 말 거예요.
상담자 다른 룸메이트를 찾아 보면 어떨까요. 제게 기숙사 방을 함께 사용할 사람을 찾는 학생들의 명단이 있어요. 아니면, 캠퍼스 외부의 숙소 목록을 살펴볼 수도 있고요.
학생 알겠어요. 두 목록을 한 부씩 가질 수 있을까요? 둘 다 찾아 보게요.
상담자 그럼요, 이걸 갖고 가세요. 행운을 빌게요!

1 남자가 여자를 찾아간 이유는 무엇인가?
(A) 다른 룸메이트를 구할 수 있을지 알아보려고
(B) 1인실을 구하려고
(C) 캠퍼스 외부의 숙소 명단을 구하려고
(D) 캠퍼스 외부의 일자리를 구하려고

정답 (B)

해설 학생이 상담자를 찾아갈 당시 원래 의도는 1인용 기숙사로 옮기는 것이었다. 이것이 불가능하게 되자 (A)나 (C)의 2차 대안을 생각해 보겠다고 한다.

2 남자의 문제는 무엇이었나?
(A) 잠을 제대로 잘 수가 없었다.
(B) 학급 친구를 찾을 수 없었다.
(C) 방을 바꿀 수가 없었다.
(D) 공부를 할 수가 없었다.

정답 (D)

해설 남학생은 룸메이트가 너무 시끄러워서 공부할 수가 없다고 한다.

ORGANIZATION
couldn't study
a noisy roommate,
a single room,
a different roommate,
off campus accommodation

Dictation for Exercise

Exercise 1
① was originally created to
② social issues
③ seems to have become
④ that makes sense
⑤ even funny
⑥ isn't really punk rock at all
⑦ it's no longer true to its origins
⑧ didn't it have to evolve
⑨ a larger audience

✓ Check-up for Expression

1. makes sense
   너는 그의 의견이 이치에 맞는다고 생각하니?

2. was created to
   그 문제를 해결하기 위해 특별위원회가 만들어졌다.

3. social issues
   이 회의의 목적은 교육이나 환경 오염 같은 사회 문제들을 토의하는 것이다.

Exercise 2
① are turning to
② as being healed by
③ treat the symptoms
④ cures the cause
⑤ an unobstructed flow of
⑥ If they are out of balance
⑦ causing illness
⑧ restores balance

✓ Check-up for Expression

1. out of balance
   보고서들은 세금 체계가 불균형하다고 경고한다.

2. is defined as
   민주주의는 종종 '국민에 의한 통치'로 정의되고 있다.

3. turn to
   그는 불과 한 달 전에 중국에서 이민을 왔기 때문에 이곳에서 의지할 만한 친구가 없다.

Exercise 3

① Fail to plan, plan to fail
② some of you want to say
③ if a market need exists
④ how long it will take
⑤ What matters is
⑥ have no budget
⑦ unwise to keep pouring
⑧ does not guarantee

✓ Check-up for Expression

1. make a profit
   이 새로운 상품으로 이윤을 창출할 수 없다면 우리 회사는 파산하게 될 것이다.

2. give up
   일단 결정을 하면 중도에서 포기하지 마라.

3. go bankrupt
   장기 경기 침체로 인해 조만간 많은 회사들이 파산하게 될 것이다.

Exercise 4

① Certainly sir
② with my dorm room
③ my roommate is too noisy
④ a single dorm available
⑤ there are none left
⑥ I'll go mad if
⑦ could try our
⑧ a copy of both lists

✓ Check-up for Expression

1. available
   내일 저녁에 회의실을 사용할 수 있을까요?

2. went mad
   컴퓨터가 또 다운되자 그는 미칠 지경이었다.

3. off campus
   대부분의 학생들이 기숙사가 아니라 캠퍼스 밖에서 산다.

Vocabulary Review

1. theme — 주제, 테마
2. perception — 인지, 인식
3. consume — 소비하다
4. vital — 치명적인, 극히 중대한
5. detect — 감지하다, 간파하다
6. beholder — 보는 사람, 구경꾼
7. anorexia — 식욕 감퇴
8. antibiotic — 항생물질
9. bulimia — 과식증, 폭식증
10. binge eating — 대식증
11. tribal — 부족의
12. infectious — 전염성의
13. supernatural — 초자연의, 불가사의한
14. constitute — 구성하다, 구성 요소가 되다
15. available — 사용[이용]할 수 있는
16. lyric — 서정시, 가사
17. primitive — 원시의, 초기의
18. acupuncture — 침술
19. symptom — 증상, 징후, 징조
20. dorm — 기숙사
21. accommodation — 숙박 설비
22. thin — 마른, 여윈
23. vomit — 토하다, 구토하다
24. empty — 비우다
25. warn — 경고하다
26. disorder — 장애, 병, 부조화
27. unobstructed — 방해받지 않은
28. opposing — 반대하는, 반하는
29. overspend — 낭비하다
30. civilization — 문명화
31. demonstrate — 증명하다, 설명하다
32. mental — 정신적인
33. make a profit — 이윤을 내다
34. out of balance — 평형을 잃고, 불안정하여
35. make sense — 이치에 닿다, 뜻이 통하다
36. no longer — 더 이상 ~ 아니다
37. sell out — 배반하다; 팔다
38. insert ~ into... — ~을 ...에 삽입하다
39. go bankrupt — 파산하다
40. deal with — 처리하다

CHAPTER 02
SUPPORTING DETAILS

Sample

생물학 수업의 강의를 듣고 물음에 답하시오.

교수 이번 강의에서는 자연이 낳은 가장 특이한 생물 가운데 하나인 아르마딜로에 대해 집중적으로 이야기하려 합니다. 이 아르마딜로를 그토록 특이한 동물로 만드는 특징은 무엇일까요? 바로 갑옷 같은 가죽입니다. 지금 어떤 사람들은 웃고 있는데, 하지만 이건 사실이예요. 이들의 몸은 철갑판 같은 뼈로 덮여 있습니다. 이 갑옷 외에도 이들은 아주 강력한 발톱을 갖추고 있죠. 이제 여러분 중에 아마 아르마딜로가 무서운 동물이고, 피해야 하는 포식 동물이라고 생각하는 사람이 있을지 모르겠군요. 그러나 사실 아르마딜로에게는 투쟁 본능이 없습니다. 이들은 굴에 사는 동물로, (동물 간의) 전투를 피해 구멍을 팝니다. 발톱이 있는 이유도 그래서입니다. 재빨리 땅을 파기 위해서 말이죠. 물론 아르마딜로가 특이한 이유는 발톱 때문도 투쟁 본능이 부족하기 때문도 아닙니다. 바로 갑옷 같은 가죽 때문에 유명한 겁니다. 어쩌면 이들을 "자연이 만들어낸 탱크"라 부를 수 있겠군요.

강의에 따르면, 다음 중 아르마딜로의 특징이 아닌 것은?
(A) 땅 속 굴에서 산다.
(B) 견고하게 보호가 되는 신체를 가지고 있다.
(C) 구멍을 능숙하게 팔 줄 안다.
(D) 날카로운 발톱으로 동물들을 공격한다.

정답 (D)

해설 강의의 세부 사항을 묻는 문제의 경우, 답안지를 하나씩 확인하면서 정답과 오답을 체크해두는 것이 좋다. 아르마딜로의 특징은 크게 '갑옷 같은 몸체, 강력한 발톱, 굴 파기'로 들 수 있다. 특히 발톱은 구멍을 파는 데 쓰이는 것이다. 이들은 전투 본능이 없다고 했으므로 (D)는 답이 되지 않는다.

Skill Check-up

Skill Check-up : 1

다음을 듣고 물음에 답하시오.

🎧 스크립트

S Excuse me! Sorry I'm late everyone… Oh! Do we have a new professor?
P No, I think you have the wrong class.
S But isn't this Room 801?
P Yes, this is Room 801 but your group is meeting in a different classroom. Your professor and I switched classrooms because I need more space for my class. There is a notice on the door if you look.
S Oh! I'm so sorry, Professor. I was in such a hurry I didn't see it.
P You need to go to Room 806, down the hall to the left. Next time, please make sure you look before you enter a room. Besides, you shouldn't be late anyway. Now, where was I?
S Yes sir, sorry, bye.

학생 실례합니다. 여러분 늦어서 죄송합니다. 아, 교수님이 바뀌었나요?
교수 아니, 학생이 강의실을 잘못 찾아왔군요.
학생 하지만, 여기가 801호 아닌가요?
교수 맞아요. 801호인 건 맞지만 학생이 속한 그룹은 다른 강의실에서 모여요. 내 수업 시간에 공간이 좀더 필요해서 학생 교수님과 강의실을 바꾸었지요. 문에 고지가 되어 있을 텐데요.
학생 아, 예, 교수님, 죄송합니다. 너무 서두르느라 보질 못했습니다.
교수 806호로 가 봐요. 복도를 따라가다가 왼쪽에 있어요. 다음에는 강의실에 들어오기 전에 반드시 살펴보도록 해요. 그리고 어쨌거나 지각을 하지 말도록 하고, 자, 어디까지 했더라?
학생 네, 교수님, 죄송합니다. 안녕히 계십시오.

교수가 강의실을 바꾼 이유는 무엇인가?
(A) 수업을 위해 더 넓은 공간이 필요했기 때문에
(B) 그의 강의실이 수리 중이기 때문에

정답 (A)

해설 수업을 진행하기 위해 좀 더 공간이 필요했다고 했다.

Word Preview

☐ **switch** (장소, 생각 등을) 바꾸다

ORGANIZATION

(d) → (c) → (b) → (a)

Check-up for Vocabulary

1. official notice 공식 공고
2. parking space 주차 공간
3. enter the house 집에 들어가다
4. switch seats 좌석을 바꾸다

다음을 듣고 물음에 답하시오.

🎧 스크립트

P You might think we are safe from the effects of pollution in this room, but are we really? Can you see the tiny specks in this ray of sunlight? They look beautfiul, don't they? But they can also be deadly. What is it that you are seeing?

S Well, isn't it just harmless dust? I remember that my grandmother used to call them 'dust angels.'

P Well, we call them particulates. What you are really seeing are small solid particles left in the air from the things we burn to support our civilization, such as wood, coal, and oil. We breathe in the remains of our civilization everyday: unburned hydrocarbons, ozone and lead.

S Now I understand why you say beautiful but deadly.

교수 여러분들은 어쩌면 우리가 이 방에 있는 한 오염의 영향으로부터 안전하다고 생각할지 모릅니다. 하지만 정말 그럴까요? 저기 태양 광선이 비추는 곳에 미세한 알갱이가 보입니까? 아름다워 보이죠? 하지만 치명적으로 위험할 수도 있습니다. 여러분이 보고 있는 것은 무엇일까요?

학생 글쎄요, 그저 무해한 먼지 아닙니까? 저희 할머니께서는 그것을 가리켜 '더스트 엔젤(먼지 천사)'이라 부르곤 하셨던 기억이 납니다.

교수 음, 우리는 그것을 미립자라고 부릅니다. 여러분들이 실제 보고 있는 것은 나무나 석탄, 석유 등, 문명을 지탱하기 위해 우리가 연소시킨 것들에서 생겨나 (소멸되지 않고) 공기 중에 남아 있는 자그마한 고체 미립자들입니다. 우리는 매일 문명의 잔해를 들이마시고 있는 셈이죠. 덜 연소된 탄화수소, 오존, 납 등을 말입니다.

학생 교수님께서 왜 그것이 아름답지만 치명적으로 위험할 수 있다고 말씀하셨는지 알겠습니다.

교수에 따르면, 미립자란 무엇인가?
(A) 오존을 형성하는 자그마한 먼지 천사의 조각
(B) 나무, 석탄, 석유 등을 연소시킨 후에 공기 중에 남아 있는 자그마한 물체

정답 (B)

해설 교수의 마지막 언급에 미립자에 대한 정의가 나와 있다. 문명을 유지하기 위해 나무, 석탄, 석유 등을 연소시킨 후에 공기 중에 남아 있는 덜 연소된 탄화수소, 오존, 납 등의 작은 고체를 뜻한다.

Word Preview

☐ **speck** 아주 작은 조각　☐ **particulate** 미립자(군)
☐ **hydrocarbon** 탄화수소　☐ **lead** 납

ORGANIZATION

(b) → (a) → (c) → (d)

Check-up for Vocabulary

1. a deadly poison 치명적인 독
2. environmental pollution 환경 오염
3. burn wood 나무를 태우다
4. harmless insects 무해한 곤충
5. feel safe 안전하다고 느끼다
6. solid shell 딱딱한 (조개) 껍질

다음을 듣고 물음에 답하시오.

🎧 스크립트

P Why do stars twinkle? Well, the reason's because their light passes through our atmosphere before it reaches us. As their light travels through the many layers of the Earth's atmosphere, it's bent many times in various directions, so it looks like the star is moving. If we went into outer space everyone would see that there are no twinkling stars. They don't move. Tonight, when we look at stars I want all of you to try an experiment. Look at the stars overhead and then at the stars close to the horizon. You should see that the stars closer to the horizon will seem to twinkle more than the ones overhead. That's because the light of the latter has to travel through more air to reach you.

교수 별이 반짝이는 이유는 무엇일까요? 그것은 별이 내보내는 빛이 우리에게 닿기 전에 대기를 통과하기 때문입니다. 별의 빛이 지구 대기의 여러 층을 통과하면서 여러 방향으로 수차례 굴절을 하게 되죠. 그래서 마치 별이 움직이는 것처럼 보입니다. 우리가 외부 우주 공간으로 나가 보면 별이 반짝거리지 않는다는 사실을 알게 될 겁니다. 별은 움직이지 않습니다. 오늘 밤, 별을 보면서 여러분 모두 한 가지 실험을 해보세요. 머리 위에 떠 있는 별을 보고, 그 다음 지평선 가까이에 있는 별을 보세요. 지평선에 더 가까운 별이 머리 위에 떠 있는 별보다 더 빛나는 것처럼 보일 것입니다. 그것은 여러분에게 닿기까지 후자의 빛이 보다 많은 공기를 통과해야 하기 때문입니다.

강의에 따르면, 별이 반짝이는 이유는 무엇인가?
(A) 별의 빛이 지구 대기에 의해 굴절되기 때문에
(B) 별이 지구 대기권 내에서 움직이기 때문에

정답 (A)

해설 별이 내보내는 빛이 대기층을 따라 움직이기 때문에 별이 움직이는 것처럼 보인다. 별 자체가 움직이는 것은 아니다.

ORGANIZATION

(d) → (a) → (b) → (c)

Check-up for Vocabulary

1. outer suburbs 교외
2. bend the body 몸을 구부리다
3. pass through a tunnel 터널을 통과하다
4. a chemical experiment 화학 실험
5. twinkle brightly 밝게 빛나다
6. in every direction 모든 방향으로

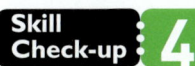

다음을 듣고 물음에 답하시오.

🎧 스크립트

P　As doctors you will have to diagnose or identify a wide range of diseases. Huntington's disease will be one of them. This is a progressive, neurological disease caused by a single gene. What are the symptoms to look for? It depends on the patient. About half of all cases start with mental symptoms such as depression. Other patients may demonstrate physical symptoms such as an unsteady walk. I'm not surprised you look worried; with symptoms like this it is very easy to misdiagnose. So, when in doubt, get a test done before you move on to other possible answers. OK! Now, let's move on to urine analysis and the role it can play in the early diagnosis of this disease.

교수 의사로서 여러분들은 광범위한 범위의 질병을 진단하고 구별해야 할 겁니다. 헌팅턴 병도 그런 질병 중의 하나가 될 것입니다. 이 병은 진행성 신경 질환으로, 한 개 유전자에 의해 발생합니다. 어떤 증상을 찾아봐야 할까요? 증상은 환자마

다 다릅니다. 환자의 반 정도는 우울증과 같은 정신적 증상으로 시작합니다. 어떤 환자들은 걸음걸이가 불안정하다든지 하는 신체적인 증상을 나타내기도 하지요. 여러분이 걱정스러운 표정을 하고 있는 것도 놀랄 일은 아닙니다. 이런 증상을 가지고는 오진하기가 쉽습니다. 때문에 뭔가 미심쩍은 경우에는 다른 진단으로 넘어가기 전에 검사를 해야 합니다. 좋아요. 이제 소변검사로 넘어가서, 소변검사가 이 헌팅턴 병의 초기 진단에 기여하는 역할에 대해 살펴보도록 합시다.

강의에 따르면, 헌팅턴 병의 증상으로 볼 수 있는 것은?
(A) 걸음걸이의 문제
(B) 배뇨 문제

정답 (A)

해설 헌팅턴 병의 증세는 사람마다 차이가 많지만 환자의 반 정도는 우울증과 같은 정신적 증상이, 어떤 사람은 비틀거리는 걸음과 같은 신체적 증상이 나타난다. 소변 검사(uninary analysis)는 병을 진단하는 테스트의 목적이지 배뇨에 문제가 있어서가 아니다.

ORGANIZATION

(a) → (b) → (d) → (c)

Check-up for Vocabulary

1. unsteady development 불안정한 발전
2. suffer from depression 우울증으로 고통 받다
3. a critical analysis 비평가의 분석
4. diagnose cancer 암을 진단하다
5. depend on the weather 날씨에 달려 있다
6. a progressive idea 진보적인 생각

Exercise

■ Exercise 1

미술 수업의 강의를 듣고 물음에 답하시오.

🎧 스크립트

P　The slide I am showing you now is *The Persistence of Memory*: perhaps one of Salvador Dali's best known works. In this oil painting Dali uses various methods to portray the effect that he wanted. For example, we have chiaroscuro. It is the use of light and shade in a picture; a bold contrast between light and dark. Another is trompe l'oeil. With this he tried to make people think that the objects are real. It is a style of painting that gives the illusion of photographic reality. Look now at the four melted clocks. They represent that time is not rigid or fixed. Note the fly on one clock reminding us that time flies; and the ants on another stating the fact that time involves decay. It raises the question; how persistent is memory really? Let's discuss that now.

ORGANIZATION
Salvador Dali,
oil,
light and dark,
rigid or fixed,
decay

교수 지금 여러분에게 보여주고 있는 슬라이드는 'The Persistence of Memory(기억의 지속)'입니다. 아마도 살바도르 달리의 작품 중에서 가장 잘 알려져 있는 작품 가운데 하나이죠. 이 유화에서 달리는 다양한 방법을 사용해서 자신이 원했던 효과를 묘사하고 있습니다. 예를 들어, 키아로스큐로(명암법)를 들 수 있겠죠. 이것은 그림 속에서 빛과 그림자를 사용하는 방법입니다. 빛과 어둠의 강렬한 대조를 이용하는 것이죠. 다른 하나는 트롱프뢰유(실물처럼 보이는 그림) 기법입니다. 이 방법을 통해 그는 사람들이 대상을 사실처럼 생각하도록 만들고자 했습니다. 이것은 그림에 사진처럼 매우 사실적인 실체라는 환상을 부여하는 기법입니다. 자, 이제 네 개의 녹아 있는 시계를 봅시다. 이 시계들은 시간이 정확하지도 고정되어 있지도 않음을 나타냅니다. 시계 하나 위에 놓여 있는 파리는 시간이 날아가듯 빠르다는 사실을 우리에게 상기시킵니다. 다른 시계 위에 놓인 개미는 시간도 부패할 수 있다는 것을 알려 줍니다. 이는 '기억이 정말로 얼마나 지속될까?'라는 질문을 제기합니다. 이제 그것에 대해 논의해 봅시다.

1 강의에 따르면, 화가가 The Persistence of Memory에서 사용한 두 가지 주요 방법은? 정답 두 개를 고르시오.
(A) 사물을 매우 사실이 아닌 것처럼 보이게 만드는 것
(B) 사물이 사진처럼 보이게 만드는 것
(C) 약한 그림자와 더 밝은 지역을 사용하는 것
(D) 강한 그림자와 더 밝은 지역을 사용하는 것

정답 (B) (D)

해설 화가가 사용했던 두 가지 방법은, 빛과 어둠의 뚜렷한 대조를 보여주는 키아로스큐로(명암법)와, 그림을 사진처럼 보이게 만드는 트롱프뢰유(실물처럼 보이는 그림)이다.

2 교수에 따르면, 녹아 있는 시계 네 개가 상징하는 것은?
(A) 우리가 보는 것을 진정으로 신뢰할 수 없다는 것
(B) 우리는 시간을 진정으로 알 수 없다는 것
(C) 시간은 계속 움직인다는 것
(D) 시간은 그림으로 그리기 힘들다는 것

정답 (C)

해설 녹아 있는 시계는 시간이 고정되지 않고 움직여 간다는 것을 나타낸다.

■ Exercise 2

패션 디자인 수업의 대화를 듣고 물음에 답하시오.

🎧 스크립트

S1 What are the most representative eras of fashion, Professor?

P I see four distinct eras shaping fashion's evolution: the 40s, feminine glamor, elegant long dresses, hats; the 50s, shirtwaist, perfectly represented in the movie *Grease* which depicts life in the 1950s; the 60s, revolution, the anti-tradition movement of the hippies; and the 70s, fun, lots of platform shoes, afroes and bell-bottoms.

S2 But what about the 80s and 90s? Don't we see lots of fashion there?

P Yes, we see lots of fashion but it's an extension of existing fashions and re-inventing fashions of the past by combining them with foreign fashions.

S2 So, you're suggesting that we have run out of genuine new ideas and since the 80s have simply been redoing the past?

P Yes, correct.

학생1 교수님, 패션의 가장 대표적인 시대는 무엇입니까?

교수 패션 발전에 현저하게 기여한 네 시기가 있습니다. 여성적인 매력, 우아하고 긴 드레스, 모자가 주를 이룬 40년대; 1950년대의 생활을 묘사했던 영화 '그리스'를 통해 완벽하게 표현된 셔츠웨이스트드레스(와이셔츠 모양으로 앞이 트인 원피스)의 시대인 50년대; 대변혁, 히피의 반전통 운동을 대변하는 60년대; 그리고 통굽 구두, 아프로 머리(흑인의 헤어스타일), 나팔식 바지가 등장하는 즐거움을 추구한 70년대입니다.

학생2 그러면 80년대와 90년대는 어떤가요? 이 시기에도 여러 패션을 볼 수 있지 않나요?

교수 네, 여러 가지 패션을 볼 수는 있지만, 이는 기존 패션의 연장으로, 외국 패션과 혼합함으로써 과거의 패션을 재창출한 것입니다.

학생2 그렇다면, 80년대 이후로는 단순히 과거를 되풀이해왔을 뿐, 우리에게는 진정으로 새로운 아이디어가 고갈되었다는 말씀이신가요?

교수 네, 그렇습니다.

1 교수에 따르면, 80년대와 90년대의 패션은 어떠한가?

(A) 상당한 변화로 재창출된 패션
(B) 과거 외국 패션의 재창출
(C) 새로운 패션으로 거듭난 과거 여러 외국 패션의 재창출
(D) 외국 패션을 사용해 재창출된 과거의 패션

정답(D)

해설 80년대와 90년대 패션은 기존 패션의 연장이면서 외국 패션과의 혼합을 통해 과거의 패션을 재창출한 형태이다. '과거'와 '외국'이라는 개념을 포함한 것을 찾는다.

2 강의에 따르면, 다음 중 사실이 아닌 것은?

(A) 패션에는 네 가지의 매우 중요한 시기가 있다.
(B) 80년대 이후로는 새로운 패션 아이디어가 없었다.
(C) 1950년대 패션의 주요 컨셉은 대변혁이다.
(D) 1940년대에는 사람들이 모자 쓰는 것을 좋아했다.

정답 (C)

해설 1950년대 패션의 주요 컨셉은 셔트웨이스트드레스이고, 대변혁은 1960년대 패션의 주요 컨셉이었다.

ORGANIZATION

Feminine Glamor,
Shirtwaist,
Revolution,
Re-invention

■ Exercise **3**

경영학 수업의 토론을 듣고 물음에 답하시오.

🎧 스크립트

P   Basically e-business means the buying and selling of goods using the Internet. Today there are millions of e-businesses on-line. Why do people buy things on-line instead of physical stores?

S1 Well, it's a matter of convenience. The users do not need to go out shopping to buy things. They can make their purchase on-line at home, office or any place where they can get connected without going out.

S2 That's right. By using the Internet, not only will it make purchasing much easier for customers, but they can also tell where to get the best quality and cheapest price by just clicking on the computer.

P   Great. OK. Then, what does it take to be successful in e-business? Let's talk about it now.

교수 기본적으로 e-비지니스는 인터넷을 통해 제품을 사고 파는 것을 의미합니다. 오늘날에는 온라인 상에 수백만 개의

e-비지니스가 성행하고 있지요. 사람들이 실제 점포를 갖고 있는 상점 대신에 온라인 상에서 물건을 사는 이유는 무엇일까요?

학생1 글쎄요, 그건 편리함의 문제일 겁니다. (온라인) 사용자들은 물건을 사러 외부로 나갈 필요가 없거든요. 집에서건 사무실에서건, 아니면 인터넷에 연결되어 있는 장소라면 어디서든지 외출하지 않고도 물건을 구입할 수 있으니까요.

학생2 맞아요. 인터넷을 사용함으로써 구매자들은 보다 쉽게 물건을 살 수 있을 뿐만 아니라 컴퓨터 상의 클릭 한 번 만으로 어디 상품이 가장 좋은지, 혹은 싼지를 알 수 있어요.

교수 좋아요. 훌륭합니다. 그러면, 이러한 e-비지니스에서 성공하기 위해서는 무엇이 필요할까요? 이제 그것에 대해 이야기해보도록 하지요.

1 교수에 따르면, e-비지니스란 무엇인가?

(A) 인터넷을 사용하여 제품을 사고 파는 것
(B) 사업체에 보다 빠르고 쉬운 인터넷 기능을 제공하는 시스템
(C) 인터넷 대신 실제 점포를 통해 물건을 거래하는 것
(D) 고객과 상인 사이의 전통적인 사업 거래

정답 (A)

해설 교수는 강의 첫머리에서 e-비지니스에 대한 정의를 내리고 학생들에게 e-비지니스가 활성화된 계기가 무엇인지를 물었다.

2 토론에 따르면, 다음 중 e-비지니스의 장점이 아닌 것은?

(A) 외출하지 않고 집에서 물건을 살 수 있다.
(B) 보다 저렴한 가격에 물건을 살 수 있다.
(C) (구매자들은) 즉각 자신이 구입한 물건의 주문 상태를 추적할 수 있다.
(D) 제품의 품질을 쉽게 비교해 볼 수 있다.

정답 (C)

해설 (C)의 경우 일반적으로는 타당한 말이나 교수와 학생들 간의 대화에서는 언급되지 않은 내용이다.

ORGANIZATION

Buying and selling of goods,
go out,
quality,
lower price

■ Exercise **4**

학생과 상담자의 대화를 듣고 물음에 답하시오.

🎧 스크립트

C   Hello! What can I do for you today?

S   I was hoping you could help me find some part-time work.

C   Yes, I can help you with that. What kind of work are you interested in?

S   I don't really want to work as a waiter or

bar tender, I'd prefer office work.

c   Well, we have several options we can look at in that area. The university library is looking for counter staff. I know that some of the labs need assistants this year, and there is always a need for student-tutors.

s   Wow! All of those sound really interesting. The work in the library would be great. How do I apply?

c   Fill in this form for me and I'll arrange an interview for you.

s   Thanks!

상담자   안녕하세요! 무엇을 도와줄까요?

학생   파트 타임 일자리 찾는 것을 도와주실 수 있는지요.

상담자   네, 도와줄 수 있어요. 어떤 종류의 일에 관심이 있나요?

학생   웨이터나 바텐더 같은 일은 정말 하고 싶지 않아요. 전 사무직 일이었으면 좋겠어요.

상담자   그 분야라면 몇 가지 살펴볼만한 안들이 있어요. 대학 도서관에서 카운터 직원을 구하고 있죠. 올해 연구 조수를 필요로 하는 연구실도 몇 군데 알고 있고요. 그리고 학생들 개인 교사에 대한 필요는 늘 있어요.

학생   와! 전부 다 재미있을 것 같네요. 그래도 도서관 일이 가장 좋겠어요. 어떻게 지원하면 되나요?

상담자   이 신청서를 작성하면 제가 면접을 주선해 드려요.

학생   고맙습니다.

1   다음 중 여자가 제시한 선택사항이 아닌 것은?

(A) 도서관 직원
(B) 조교
(C) 학생 개인 교사
(D) 연구실 조교

정답 (B)

2   여자의 말에 따르면, 남자는 어떻게 자신이 원하는 직업에 지원할 수 있는가?

(A) 신청서를 작성한다.
(B) 면접을 보기 위해 편지를 쓴다.
(C) 도서관에서 면접을 본다.
(D) 여자에게 편지를 쓴다.

정답 (A)

해설   먼저 신청서를 작성한 후, 면접을 한다. 단, 면접 주선자는 상담원이다.

ORGANIZATION

part-time work,
counter staff at the library,
student tutor,
assistant at the lab,
fill in the form / have an interview

Dictation for Exercise

Exercise 1

① The slide I am showing
② In this oil painting
③ various methods to portray
④ a bold contrast between light and dark
⑤ is not rigid
⑥ Note the fly on one clock
⑦ It raises the question

✓ Check-up for Expression

1. try to
   이 일을 이달 말까지 끝내 주십시오.
2. a style of
   글을 쓸 때는 자기만의 스타일을 만드는 것이 중요하다.
3. stale
   그가 먼저 요청하지 않는다면 네 의견을 말하지 마라.

Exercise 2

① representative eras of
② four distinct eras shaping
③ depicts life in the 1950s
④ it's an extension of
⑤ by combining them with
⑥ have run out of genuine new ideas
⑦ been redoing the past

✓ Check-up for Expression

1. ran out of
   우리는 일 마일도 더 갈 수 없었다. 기름이 다 떨어졌다.
2. combines with
   수소는 산소와 결합하여 물을 생성한다.
3. an extension of
   저는 마감일을 연장하는 문제에 관한 답을 얻고 싶습니다.

Exercise 3

① the buying and selling of goods
② instead of physical stores
③ it's a matter of
④ on-line at home, office or any place
⑤ get connected
⑥ much easier for customers
⑦ what does it take to

✔Check-up for Expression

1. instead of
   너는 비행기 대신 기차를 타는 가능성을 고려해봐야 할 것 같다.
2. a matter of
   그것이 어렵다고 하는 게 아니다. 그것은 단지 흥미의 문제이다.
3. get connected
   그 정보를 얻고 싶다면 먼저 인터넷에 연결되어 있어야 한다.

Exercise 4

① I was hoping
② are you interested in
③ I'd prefer
④ in that area
⑤ some of the labs
⑥ there is always a need for
⑦ Fill in this form
⑧ I'll arrange an interview

✔Check-up for Expression

1. fill in
   그 경기에 참가하고 싶다면 먼저 이 서류를 작성해 주세요.
2. arragne
   그 문제에 관해 토론하기 위해서는 마케팅 팀과의 회의를 마련해야 한다.
3. help with
   우리 위원회는 학생들이 겪고 있는 여러 문제들을 돕기 위해 생겨난 것이다.

Vocabulary Review

No.	Word	Meaning
1.	era	시대, 시기
2.	space	공간, 장소
3.	enter	들어가다, 입장하다
4.	notice	공고, 공지
5.	speck	아주 작은 조각
6.	particulate	미립자(군)
7.	symptom	증상, 증후
8.	lead	납
9.	gene	유전자, 유전 인자
10.	elegant	우아한, 기품 있는
11.	switch	(장소, 생각 등을) 바꾸다
12.	reinvention	재발명, 재창조
13.	application	신청서, 지원서
14.	deadly	치명적인, 치사의
15.	pollution	오염
16.	burn	타다; 태우다
17.	harmless	무해한, 해가 없는
18.	safe	안전한
19.	twinkle	반짝이다, 빛나다
20.	direction	방향; 지시
21.	analysis	분석, 검토
22.	horizon	지평선, 수평선
23.	progressive	진행하는; 진보하는
24.	neurological	신경의, 신경학상의
25.	depression	우울, 의기소침
26.	urine	오줌, 소변
27.	portray	그리다, 묘사하다
28.	diagnose	(병을) 진단하다
29.	unsteady	불안정한, 불규칙한
30.	arrange	마련하다, 준비하다
31.	atmosphere	대기, 공기
32.	pass through ~	~을 통과하다, ~을 지나다
33.	raise a question	문제를 제기하다
34.	combine with ~	~와 결합하다
35.	run out of ~	~이 바닥나다, ~을 다 써버리다
36.	instead of ~	~ 대신에
37.	depend on ~	~에 의존하다, ~에 달려있다
38.	a matter of ~	~에 관한 문제
39.	get connected	(컴퓨터에) 연결되다
40.	without ~ing	~하지 않고, ~ 없이

CHAPTER 03
PROCESS / CLASSIFICATION

Sample

생물학 수업의 강의를 듣고 물음에 답하시오.

교수 우리는 이번 강의들을 통해 '인간은 동물인가?'라는 물음에 대해 토론해왔습니다. 오늘 강의는 인간과 유인원 사이에 존재하는 차이점에 중점을 두겠습니다. 우선 움직임, 신체적 구조 등의 요소를 살펴보겠습니다. 자, 움직임에 대해 말하자면, 인간은 두 발 동물입니다. 다시 말하면 우리 인간은 직립 자세로 걷지요. 영장류도 직립 자세로 걸을 때가 있지만, 여러분이 알고 있듯이 보통은 팔 다리 모두를 사용해서 걷습니다. 신체 구조 또한 다릅니다. 인간의 척추는 독특하게도 'S' 형이지만, 영장류의 척추는 둥근 아치형입니다. 또 하나 특이한 면은, 인간의 손이 더 짧고 더 넓으며 근육이 더 많이 붙어 있다는 사실입니다. 결과적으로 인간의 손은 영장류나 다른 동물보다 더 강하고 더 정밀합니다.

이 강의에서 교수는 인간과 영장류의 차이점에 대해 설명하였다. 각 항목에 대한 올바른 설명을 찾아 표시하시오.

	인간	유인원
그들은 직립 자세로 걷는다.	✓	
그들의 척추는 둥근 아치 형이다.		✓
그들은 주로 네 발로 움직인다.		✓
그들 손에는 근육이 더 많이 붙어 있다.	✓	

해설 인간 – 직립 자세 / S형 척추 / 짧고 넓은 손, 더 많은 근육으로 정밀한 움직임을 보인다.
영장류 – 네발로 걷기 / 둥근 아치형 척추 / 손의 경우, 인간과 영장류를 비교한 점으로 짐작 가능하다.

Skill Check-up

Skill Check-up : 1

다음을 듣고 물음에 답하시오.

 스크립트

P Memory is an information process, somewhat similar to a computer information-processing system: though by no means identical. First we use an encoding process; which is getting information into our brain, to obtain information. And then we retain that information like a computer memory.

We store a great deal of information in our long-term memory. Finally we get the information back when needed by retrieving information. However, humans also possess short-term memory. This is activated memory holding information for only a brief time, such as phone numbers needed when dialing. If such information does not pass to the long-term memory it is rapidly lost.

교수 (인간의) 기억이란 정보 처리 과정으로, 완전히 똑같지는 않지만 어느 정도 컴퓨터의 정보 처리 체계와 유사합니다. 먼저 우리는 부호화 과정을 사용합니다. 부호화 과정은 정보를 얻기 위해 우리 뇌로 정보를 가져오는 것을 의미하지요. 그런 다음, 우리는 컴퓨터 메모리처럼 정보를 간직해 둡니다. 우리는 이 많은 양의 정보를 장기 기억으로 저장해 둡니다. 마지막으로 우리는 검색을 통해 필요할 때마다 이들 정보를 꺼내 오는 것이죠. 그런데 인간은 또한 단기 기억이라는 것도 가지고 있습니다. 이것은 활성 기억이라는 것으로 아주 짧은 기간 동안만 정보를 간직하는 것입니다. 전화를 해야할 때 전화번호를 기억하는 것처럼 말이죠. 이런 기억들은 장기 기억으로 옮겨 가지 않을 경우 금새 잊혀지는 것들입니다.

다음 설명이 정보 처리 과정을 나타내는지 표시하시오.

	예	아니오
우리는 컴퓨터처럼 정보를 암호로 바꾸어 저장한다.	✓	
우리는 컴퓨터 메모리처럼 정보를 보유한다.	✓	
우리는 단기 기억 속에 정보를 저장한다.		✓
우리의 필요할 때마다 정보를 꺼내온다.	✓	

해설 우리가 정보를 저장하는 방법은 정보를 암호화해서 장기 기억에 저장하는 것이다. 단기 기억이란 일시적으로 정보를 보유하고 있는 것으로 장기 기억으로 전환되지 않을 경우 기억에서 사라진다.

Word Preview

☐ **encode** 암호[부호]화하다　　☐ **retrieve** 되찾다, (정보를) 검색하다
☐ **retain** 간직하다, 유지하다

ORGANIZATION

(d) → (c) → (e) → (b) → (a)

Check-up for Vocabulary

1. a brief note 짤막한 편지
2. encode data 정보를 부호화하다
3. take a great deal of time 시간을 많이 소비하다
4. obtain great fame 대단한 명성을 얻다
5. store food for the winter 겨울을 대비해 식량을 저장하다
6. a long-term contract 장기 계약

Skill Check-up : 2

다음을 듣고 물음에 답하시오.

 스크립트

P There have been two major theories for the universe's origins; Big Bang and Steady State. The Big Bang theory suggests the universe had a beginning, starting with a huge explosion. The Steady State theory suggests that the universe did not begin, that it has always existed. Also, the Big Bang universe is a place that's significantly different today from what it was before. As we move outwards from the center of the universe we find items such as quasars that appear to have only recently come into existence. Whereas in the Steady State universe things have always been the same and therefore there's nothing new.

S So... which theory is more accepted?

P For many years Steady State was the leading theory but now Big Bang is dominant.

교수 우주의 기원에 관한 두 가지 주요 이론이 있습니다. 빅뱅 이론과 정상 우주론이 그것입니다. 빅뱅 이론은 우주가 커다란 폭발과 함께 시작되었다는 이론입니다. 정상 우주론은 우주가 시작이란 것이 없이 (원래부터) 항상 존재해왔다는 이론입니다. 또한 빅뱅 우주는 과거의 모습과 오늘날의 모습이 현저히 다릅니다. 우주의 중심에서 바깥쪽으로 나가보면, 최근에야 존재해온 것으로 보이는 준성과 같은 물체를 발견하게 되지요. 반면에 정상 우주론의 우주에서 사물은 언제나 동일하기 때문에 새로운 것이란 없습니다.

학생 그렇다면... 어떤 이론이 좀더 통설로 받아들여지고 있나요?

교수 오랜 세월 동안 정상 우주론이 주도적인 이론이었지만 지금은 빅뱅 이론이 지배적입니다.

각 이론에 대해 옳게 설명한 항목에 표시하시오.

	빅뱅 이론	정상 우주론
우주는 결코 변하지 않았다.		✔
우주는 이 사건에서 비롯됐다.	✔	
과학자는 현재 이 이론을 선호한다.	✔	
우주는 영원하다.		✔

해설 빅뱅 이론은 우주가 커다란 폭발과 함께 시작되었다는 것으로 현재 지배적인 이론이다. 반면에 정상 우주론은 우주란 새로운 것이 없어 늘 존재해왔던 영원한 존재라 주장한다.

Word Preview

☐ **explosion** 폭발, 파열   ☐ **dominant** 지배적인, 우세한

ORGANIZATION

(a) → (b) → (c) → (d)

Check-up for Vocabulary

1. a news item 뉴스 아이템
2. a huge ship 거대한 배
3. travel outwards into space 우주로 여행하다
4. the dominant party 제 1 당(다수당)
5. a leading businessman 일류(손꼽히는) 사업가
6. the origin of the civilization 문명의 기원

Skill Check-up : 3

다음을 듣고 물음에 답하시오.

🎧 스크립트

P So everyone, just where did lacrosse come from? Well, believe it or not, it was invented by Native Americans. Two of the main Indian tribes that participated in this sport were... the Cherokee and the Iroquois. The Cherokees used it as a form of military training but for the Iroquois it was simply a game. The former had teams consisting of hundreds, sometimes thousands of players. The goals were miles apart and games could last hours or even days. Players focused more on injuring their opponents with their sticks than hitting the ball. By comparison the Iroquois had a very organized and more sports orientated game. Teams consisted of only 12 to 15 players each and the goals were only about 120 feet apart.

교수 그렇다면 여러분, 라크로스(10 명을 한 팀으로 하는, 그물 모양의 라켓을 사용한 하키 비슷한 게임)는 어디에서 유래되었을까요? 믿기 힘들지도 모르지만, 이것은 미국 원주민들이 처음으로 고안했습니다. 이 스포츠에 참여했던 주요 인디언 부족 중 두 부족은 체로키 족과 이로쿼이 족이었습니다. 체로키 족은 이 스포츠를 군사 훈련의 한 형태로 사용했지만, 이로쿼이 족은 단순히 경기로 사용했습니다. 체로키 족은 수백, 수 천 명의 선수들로 팀을 구성하였습니다. 골대는 수 마일 떨어져 있었고, 경기는 몇 시간, 심지어는 며칠 동안 계속되었습니다. 선수들은 볼을 치기보다 스틱을 가지고 상대방에게 부상을 입히는 데 더욱 치중했지요. 이와는 대조적으로 이로쿼이 족은 매우 조직적이고 좀 더 스포츠 지향적인 경기를 했습니다. 팀은 각각 12~15명 정도로만 구성되었고, 골대도 겨우 120 피트 정도만 떨어져 있을 뿐이었습니다.

각 부족에 대한 올바른 설명에 표시하시오.

	체로키	이로쿼이
그것은 전쟁을 대비한 중요한 경기였다.	✔	
선수들은 스틱을 사용해 상대방 선수들을 부상 입혔다.	✔	
그것은 매우 잘 조직되었다.		✔
골대는 단지 120 피트 정도만 떨어져 있었다.		✔

해설 체로키 족은 라크로스를 군사훈련의 한 형태로 생각하였다. 볼을 쳐서 점수를 내는 것보다 스틱으로 상대방을 공격하는 데 중점을 두었다. 반면 이로쿼이 족은 좀 더 조직적으로 스포츠답게 경기를 치러서 선수 구성원도 적고 골대까지 거리도 짧았다.

ORGANIZATION

(a) → (b) → (d) → (e) → (c)

Check-up for Vocabulary

1. an African tribe 아프리카 부족
2. last for 3 hours 3시간 동안 지속되다
3. injure your health 건강을 해치다
4. participate in management 경영에 참여하다
5. a well organized group 잘 조직된 단체
6. professional training 전문적인(직업) 훈련

Skill Check-up 4

다음을 듣고 물음에 답하시오.

🎧 스크립트

S1 I want to join a school activity club, maybe football or baseball.
S2 Well, if you want to do that then you have to try out. You can't just join those clubs. You need to prove you are good enough to be on the team.
S1 How do I do that?
S2 First you take a medical; then you join Saturday training with the team.
S1 Join training with the team?
S2 Yes, it's for the coach. You have to play in a practice game and the coach watches and decides if you are good enough.
S1 So I have to be fit then?
S2 Yes, boys have to be very fit to get on those teams. Why not join my workout club first and get fit?

S1 But I thought your club was only for girls.
S2 Oh no! Boys can join, too!

학생1 학교 운동 클럽에 들고 싶어. 미식 축구나 야구부 말이야.
학생2 음, 그렇게 하고 싶다면, 팀 선발에 나가 봐. 그런 클럽에 그냥 들어갈 수는 없잖아. 그 팀에 속할 만큼 잘 한다는 점을 증명할 필요가 있어.
학생1 어떻게 하면 되지?
학생2 우선, 건강 진단을 받아야 해. 그런 다음 토요일에 있는 팀 훈련에 합류하는 거야.
학생1 팀 훈련에 참가하라고?
학생2 그래, 코치에게 보여야 하니까. 연습 게임에 참가해서 운동을 해야 해. 그러면 코치가 그걸 보고 네가 팀에 합류할 만큼 잘 하는지 판단하게 돼.
학생1 그러면 몸이 좋아야야겠지?
학생2 그럼, 그런 팀에 들어가려는 사람들은 아주 몸이 좋아야 해. 일단 우리 헬스 클럽에 가입해서 몸을 만드는 것이 어때?
학생1 하지만, 네 클럽은 여학생만 가입하는 곳인 줄 알았는데.
학생2 아니야! 남학생들도 가입할 수 있어.

다음 설명이 옳은지 틀린지 표시하시오.

팀 가입하기	예	아니오
매우 건강해야 한다.	✔	
팀 선수들과 먼저 운동을 해 봐야 한다.	✔	
얼마나 능숙하게 경기를 할 수 있는지 보여 주어야 한다.	✔	
헬스 클럽에 가입해야 한다.		✔
필기 시험에 통과해야 한다.		✔

해설 팀에 가입하려면 진찰을 받아 신체가 건강함을 증명하고, 팀 구성원과 연습경기를 해서 실력을 인정 받아야 한다. 필기 시험에 대한 언급은 없고, 헬스 클럽에 합류하는 것은 클럽 가입 조건을 충족시키기 위해 여학생이 제시한 의견이지 필수 사항이 아니다.

ORGANIZATION

(c) → (b) → (a) → (d)

Check-up for Vocabulary

1. join a club 클럽에 가입하다
2. prove the innocence 결백을 증명하다
3. a total-body workout 전신 운동
4. have a medical check-up 건강 진단을 받다

Exercise

■ Exercise 1

정치학 수업의 대화를 듣고 물음에 답하시오.

🎧 스크립트

P How does one become President of the United States? First, party members get to vote for the candidate that will represent their party in the upcoming general election. And then the people vote for one candidate. However, when people cast a vote, they are not voting directly for an individual Presidential candidate. Voters in each state actually cast their vote for a group of people which we say is the Electoral College.

S What's the Electoral College?

P It is a system in which each state has as many electors as it has representatives and senators. And these electors cast their votes for their state's preferred candidate. Candidates who win this general election in a state secure all that state's electoral votes. If a candidate wins 270 or more of the electoral votes then they become president.

교수 미국의 대통령은 어떻게 되는 걸까요? 먼저, 당에서 차기 총선거에서 자기 당을 대표할 후보를 뽑습니다. 그러면 국민들이 그 중 한 후보에게 투표를 하는 것이죠. 그러나 이들이 투표를 할 때는 각 대통령 후보에게 직접 투표를 하는 것은 아닙니다. 각 주의 유권자들은 특정 그룹에게 표를 던지는데, 이들을 대통령 선거인단이라고 합니다.

학생 대통령 선거인단이 무엇인가요?

교수 이것은 각 주가 그 주의 상·하원 의원 수만큼의 선거인을 갖게 되는 시스템이에요. 이들 선거인들이 각 주의 주민들이 가장 선호하는 후보에게 표를 던지는 겁니다. 이 총선거에서 승리한 후보가 그 주의 모든 표를 차지하게 되죠. 한 후보가 선거인단의 표 가운데 270 표 이상을 획득할 경우, 이 후보가 대통령이 됩니다.

1 각 설명이 사실인지 여부를 표시하시오.

	예	아니오
당에서 자기 당을 대표할 후보를 선출한다.	✔	
대통령 선거인은 차기 대통령 감에게 투표를 한다.	✔	
각 주의 주민이 직접 대통령을 선출한다.		✔
선거인단은 대통령을 선출하는 방식이다.	✔	

해설 1) 각 정당이 대통령 후보자를 지명하면, 2) 각 주의 유권자가 대통령 선거인을 선출하고, 3) 이렇게 선출된 대통령 선거인이 자신이 속한 주를 대표해서 대통령 후보에게 표를 던진다. 여기서 270 표 이상을 획득한 후보가 대통령이 된다.

2 교수에 따르면, 대통령 선거인단은 무엇인가?

(A) 투표하는 방법을 배우는 방식
(B) 각 주의 인기 있는 후보들
(C) 대통령을 선출하는 최상의 방법
(D) 대통령 후보에게 투표하는 선거인들

정답 (D)

ORGANIZATION

Presidential election,
select a candidate,
for electors,
Electoral College,
with 270 or more votes

■ Exercise 2

교수와 학생의 대화를 듣고 물음에 답하시오.

🎧 스크립트

S What is our assignment for this class?

P You have two options; you can either write an essay or compose a poem. If you write a poem you will be required to produce an original work that has the following elements: it's in blank verse; it's an expression of your own thoughts on grace; and is no more than 300 words long.

S Okay. What about the essay?

P If you choose the essay option then I want to see a review of the current academic literature discussing grace; the paper must be between 2,000 and 2,500 words; and I also expect a full bibliography.

S When is the deadline?

P You have to hand it in before our last lesson.

S Wow! That's only two weeks away. I'm definitely going to choose the essay because it would take me at least a month to write a poem!

학생 이번 수업의 과제물은 무엇입니까?

교수 두 가지 선택사항이 있습니다. 평론을 쓰거나 시를 쓰는 겁니다. 시를 쓰는 경우에는, 다음의 요소를 포함하는 독창적인 작품을 써야 합니다. 즉 무운시여야 하고, 신의 은총에 대한 자신의 생각을 표현해야 하고, 300 단어를 초과하지 않아야 합니다.

학생 알겠습니다. 평론은요?
교수 평론을 쓸 때는, 신의 은총을 논한 현대 논문을 비평하세요. 분량은 2,000~2,500 자여야 하고, 참고 문헌 목록을 기록하세요.
학생 제출기한은 언제입니까?
교수 마지막 수업 시간 전에 제출해야 합니다.
학생 예? 2 주밖에 남질 않았네요. 시를 쓰려면 최소한 한 달은 걸릴 테니 아무래도 평론을 써야겠습니다.

1 다음 설명이 알맞은 곳에 표시하시오.

	시	에세이
무운시로 써야 한다.	✔	
신의 은총에 대한 학문적 문학 토론을 검토해야 한다.		✔
300 단어 미만을 사용해야 한다.	✔	
작품의 출처를 밝혀야 한다.		✔

2 교수는 제출 기한에 대해 무엇이라고 하는가?

(A) 완성했을 때 제출한다.
(B) 완성하기까지 2 주 남았다.
(C) 이달 말 이전에 끝내야 한다.
(D) 마지막 수업 이후에 제출할 수 있다.

정답 (B)

해설 교수의 말에 따르면, 과제물은 마지막 수업 이전에 제출해야 하고, 앞으로 2주 남았다.

ORGANIZATION

blank verse,
300 words,
grace,
2,000~2,500 words,
bibliography,
before last lesson

■ Exercise 3

건축학 수업의 대화를 듣고 물음에 답하시오.

🎧 스크립트

P Both the temple and the cathedral are two different types of religious architecture. Let's compare *The Temple of Srirangam* with *The Abbey of St. Denis*. The Srirangam temple was built for the people. Serving as a community center, through various rituals, it preserved moral values among the masses. The abbey, though a church, was focused on the select few, in this case royalty.

S So the abbey in this case is more political rather than religious in purpose.

P What we're talking about here is the purpose for the architecture. One was designed to glorify the monarch but the other was primarily built to benefit the whole community.

S So then, that means... the temple serves society and the abbey primarily serves royalty?

P Correct! The temple is more practical in design, being a place for the people but the abbey is designed to create awe, respect and reverence for French royalty.

교수 사원과 대성당은 두 가지 다른 형태의 종교 건축물입니다. 스리랑감 사원과 성 데니스 수도원을 비교해 봅시다. 스리랑감 사원은 민중을 위해 건축되었습니다. 공동체의 중심 역할을 하며, 다양한 의식을 통해 일반 대중 사이에 도덕적 가치를 보존했지요. 성 데니스 수도원은 교회임에도 불구하고 선택된 소수에 보다 중심을 두었습니다. 이 경우에는 왕족이라고 할 수 있겠군요.
학생 그렇다면 이 경우의 수도원은 그 목적에 있어서 종교적이라기 보다는 정치적이라는 거군요.
교수 우리가 이 시간에 말하고 있는 것은 건축물의 목적입니다. 하나는 군주를 예찬하기 위해 건축되었고, 다른 하나는 전체 지역 사회에 혜택을 주는 것을 주 목적으로 건축되었습니다.
학생 그렇다면 그 말씀은... 사원은 사회에 봉사하고 수도원은 주로 왕족에 봉사한다는 뜻인가요?
교수 정확해요. 사원은 설계상으로 보다 실용적이고 민중을 위한 장소였던 반면, 사원은 프랑스 왕족들에 대한 경탄과, 존경, 숭배를 끌어내기 위한 목적으로 설계되었습니다.

1 각 항목과 일치하는 설명을 찾아 표시하시오.

	사원	수도원
지역사회에 봉사한다.	✔	
왕족에게 보다 중요하다.		✔
군주를 예찬하기 위해 건축되었다.		✔
보다 실용적인 디자인이다.	✔	

해설 스리랑감 사원은 대중을 위한 장소로, 다양한 의식을 통해 공동체의 중심 역할을 담당했다. 즉, 사회 봉사라는 목적에 충실하기 위해 실용적인 디자인으로 설계되었다. 반면에 성 데니스 수도원은 선택된 왕족이라는 소수 계층에 봉사하기 위해 설계되었다.

2 교수에 따르면, 다음 중 사실인 것은?

(A) 사원은 전체 지역 사회 중심을 두고 있다.
(B) 수도원은 지역 공동체의 회합 장소이다.
(C) 둘 다 정부의 필요를 충족시킨다.
(D) 둘 다 프랑스에 중요하다.

정답 (A)

해설 사원은 전체 지역 사회에 봉사하지만 대성당 (혹은 수도원)은 선택된 소수에게만 봉사한다.

ORGANIZATION

political,
royalty,
the monarch,
religious,
people,
the whole community

■ Exercise4

과학 수업의 강의를 듣고 물음에 답하시오.

🎧 스크립트

P Sometimes gigantic waves occur in the oceans of the world. Some of you listening might know this phenomenon by the name 'tidal wave', yes? But the preferred term in modern times is the word 'tsunami', which means 'harbor wave.' Many scientists use this name because tides, which are caused by the moon, do not create these massive waves. There are many different causes for tsunamis. They can be caused by landslides, volcanoes, eruptions and explosions of various kinds, but the most common cause is earthquakes. When earthquakes occur, part of the sea floor suddenly moves upward and part suddenly sinks downwards. Immediately after this happens the sea's surface tries to copy the shape of the sea floor. Gravity begins to take control and tries to return the sea's surface back to its original shape. As this occurs, the ragged sea begins to race outwards, and tries to become evenly spaced again. At that moment a tsunami is born.

교수 때로 세계에 존재하는 해양에서 거대한 파도가 발생하기도 하지요. 여러분 중에 어떤 사람들은 이 현상을 해일이라는 이름으로 알고 있을지도 모르겠군요, 그렇죠? 하지만 현대에 선호되는 용어는 '쓰나미'라는 단어입니다. '항만 파도'를 뜻하지요. 많은 과학자들이 이 이름을 사용합니다. 그것은

이 거대한 파도를 만들어 내는 것이 달에 의해 발생되는 조류가 아니기 때문입니다. 쓰나미가 발생하는 데는 여러 가지 원인이 있습니다. 산사태, 화산, 다양한 종류의 분출과 폭발이 그 원인입니다. 하지만, 가장 보편적인 원인은 지진이예요. 지진이 발생하면 해저의 일부가 갑자기 솟아오르고 일부는 갑자기 아래로 가라앉게 되죠. 이런 일이 발생한 직후에 해수면은 해저의 모습을 그대로 따라가려는 성향을 보입니다. 그러면 중력이 작용하면서 해수면을 이전 상태로 돌려 놓으려고 합니다. 이렇게 되면 들쭉날쭉한 바다는 다시 원래와 같은 고른 상태를 유지하려고 밖을 향해서 돌진하기 시작합니다. 바로 이때 쓰나미가 탄생하는 겁니다.

1 다음 설명이 쓰나미의 발생 과정인지 표시하시오.

	예	아니오
종종 지진이 쓰나미를 발생시킨다.	✔	
조류는 주요 쓰나미 발생 원인의 하나이다.		✔
달이 지면 바다가 갑자기 거대한 파도를 만들어낸다.		✔
해양의 표면은 해저의 모습을 본뜨려고 한다.	✔	
중력이 바다의 표면을 원래 모습으로 돌아오게 한다.	✔	

해설 지진은 쓰나미 발생원인 중 하나이다. 지진이 일어나 해저가 들쭉날쭉해지면 바다 표면은 해저의 이런 모습을 따라가려 한다. 이때 중력이 작용해서 바다의 표면을 예전의 모습으로 돌려놓으려고 하고, 이런 충돌 속에서 쓰나미가 발생한다. 달에 의한 조류가 쓰나미를 발생시키는 것은 아니다.

2 교수에 따르면, 쓰나미는 무엇인가?

(A) 자연 항만을 만들어내는 매우 거대한 파도
(B) 자연 항만을 파괴하는 매우 커다란 파도
(C) 항만을 채우는 매우 커다란 파도
(D) 항만으로 밀려 오는 매우 거대한 파도

정답 (D)

해설 쓰나미는 '항만 파도'로 거대한 파도가 항만으로 밀려 오기 때문에 붙여진 명칭이다.

ORGANIZATION

harbor wave,
earthquakes,
sea floor,
gravity

Dictation for Exercise

Exercise 1 --
① get to vote for
② in the upcoming
③ they are not voting
④ in each state

⑤ in which each state has
⑥ as it has
⑦ for their state's preferred candidate
⑧ secure all that

✔ Check-up for Expression

1. presidential election
   그는 차기 대선 후보이다.
2. Voters
   유권자들은 보수당 후보들에게 투표했다.
3. secure
   우리는 언론의 자유를 보장받아야 한다.

Exercise 2

① either write an essay
② you will be required to
③ it's in blank verse
④ see a review of
⑤ When is the deadline
⑥ hand it in
⑦ I'm definitely going to choose
⑧ at least a month

✔ Check-up for Expression

1. hand in
   (작성한) 딕테이션을 지금 바로 제출하시오.
2. are required to
   대학 추천을 받으려면 80 점 이상을 받아야 한다.
3. review of
   그 시에 대한 평론은 아주 비판적이었다.

Exercise 3

① Serving as a community center
② among the masses
③ though a church
④ in purpose
⑤ designed to glorify
⑥ was primarily built to benefit
⑦ in design
⑧ is designed to create awe

✔ Check-up for Expression

1. rather than
   그는 옛날 고전 작품을 읽는 것보다 현대시를 읽는 것을 좋아한다.
2. focus on
   오늘 토론은 고용인들의 업무 능력 고취 방법론에 대한 것이다.
3. serve as
   우리는 영어 교사를 할 사람을 구하고 있다.

Exercise 4

① occur in
② might know
③ the preferred term
④ which are caused by
⑤ moves upward
⑥ sinks downwards
⑦ the sea's surface tries to
⑧ the sea's surface back to
⑨ become evenly spaced

✔ Check-up for Expression

1. occur in
   대부분의 태풍은 태평양 지역에서 발생한다.
2. caused by
   때때로 사람들은 자신들이 섭취한 음식물 때문에 병에 걸리기도 한다.
3. return to
   연어는 알을 낳기 위해 자신이 태어난 장소로 돌아가는 것으로 알려져 있다.

Vocabulary Review

1. glorify	찬미하다, 영광을 찬양하다
2. retain	간직하다, 유지하다
3. tribe	부족, 종족
4. upcoming	곧 다가오는
5. medical	건강 진단, 진료
6. store	저장하다
7. long-term	장기의
8. brief	짧은, 단시간의
9. explosion	폭발, 파열
10. dominant	지배적인, 우세한
11. consist	되어[이루어져] 있다
12. opponent	적수, 상대
13. origin	기원
14. huge	거대한
15. leading	이끄는, 선도하는
16. retrieve	되찾다, (정보를) 검색하다
17. training	훈련
18. last	지속하다
19. injure	다치게 하다, 부상입히다
20. organized	조직된, 계획된
21. obtain	얻다, 획득하다
22. fit	컨디션이 좋은; 적임의
23. spine	척추
24. device	장치, 고안
25. representative	(미) 국회의원, 하원
26. senator	상원 의원
27. bibliography	관계 서적 목록
28. abbey	대수도원, 대성당
29. encode	암호[부호]화하다
30. monarch	군주, 제왕

31. the masses	일반 대중, 서민
32. win votes	표를 얻다
33. cast a vote	투표하다
34. either A or B	A 나 B 가운데 하나는
35. hand in	제출하다
36. a great deal of ~	대단히 많은 ~
37. participate in ~	~에 참가하다
38. focus on ~	~에 초점을 맞추다
39. serve as ~	~의 역할을 하다
40. in this case	이러한 경우에

CHAPTER 04
ORGANIZATION

Sample

과학 수업의 대화를 듣고 물음에 답하시오.

교수 우리가 계속해서 다양한 기상 현상에 대해 살펴보고 있는데, 오늘은 토네이도에 대해 토론해 보겠습니다. 여러분의 교재 32쪽을 펴면 활동 상태의 토네이도 사진을 볼 수 있습니다. 자세하게 살펴보고 이 사진들 대부분이 어디에서 찍힌 것인지 말해 보세요.

학생 미국인가요?

교수 네, 그렇습니다. 자 그럼 이 교재에서 미국의 모습이 이렇게 두드러진 이유는 무엇일까요?

학생 토네이도의 대부분이 미국에서 발생하기 때문입니다.

교수 맞습니다. 미국은 매년 평균 800건의 토네이도가 발생하는 세계 제 1의 토네이도 발생국입니다. 이는 미국이 캐나다에서 불어오는 건조한 공기와 멕시코 만에서 발생한 차가운 습기를 차단할 산맥이 부족하기 때문입니다.

교수는 미국에서 발생하는 토네이도를 어떤 방식으로 설명하는가?

(A) 캐나다의 토네이도 발생 수치와 비교함으로써
(B) 교재에 나와있는 미국 토네이도의 특징을 설명함으로써
(C) 빈번한 토네이도 발생의 이유를 지적함으로써
(D) 미국 토네이도가 어떻게 형성되는지 설명함으로써

정답 (C)

해설 미국이 매년 800 건이나 되는 토네이도가 발생하는 것은 캐나다에서 오는 건조한 공기와 멕시코 만에서 발생한 차가운 습기를 차단할 산악지대가 부족하기 때문이라며 그 이유를 설명하고 있다.

Skill Check-up

Skill Check-up : 1

다음을 듣고 물음에 답하시오.

 스크립트

S Incidents of children being violent are increasing because of our media becoming more violent. Children are imitating what they see.

P Actually, none of the studies confirm a link between them. Even if studies did demonstrate a link, we still wouldn't know what kind of media violence really matters. You might read the UCLA study. It demonstrates just how complex this issue has become. They had to cover so much: serious concerns on brutally violent movies or films: violent media that raises less concern: and low level violence causing concern because it treats violence as a joke. Which of these, if any, really are genuine causes for concern, has yet to be determined. There are no simple answers to this question.

학생 대중 매체가 더욱 폭력적이 되면서 아이들이 폭력적으로 되는 경우 역시 증가하고 있습니다. 아이들은 그들이 (매체를 통해) 보는 것들을 모방하고 있는 것입니다.

교수 실제로 이 두 가지 사이에 관련이 있다는 사실을 입증한 연구는 없습니다. 연구를 통해 그 관련성이 드러난다 하더라도, 사실 진정 문제가 되고 있는 매체가 무엇인지는 여전히 알 수 없을 겁니다. 여러분도 UCLA 연구 결과를 살펴 보았을지 모르겠군요. 이 연구에서는 이같은 주제가 얼마나 복잡한 것인지를 여실히 보여줍니다. 이들은 너무도 많은 사항들을 다루어야 했습니다. 대단히 폭력적인 영화들, 우려를 덜 자아내긴 하지만 폭력적인 매체, 그리고 폭력을 장난처럼 다루기 때문에 우려를 자아내는 낮은 수준의 폭력들 같은 심각한 문제들을 말이죠. 이것 중 어느 것이 우려해야만 하는 진정한 원인인지는 아직 판가름나지 않았습니다. 이 질문에 대한 답은 간단하지 않습니다.

교수는 미디어와 그 폭력성을 어떤 방식으로 설명하는가?

(A) 아이들의 몇 가지 폭력 사례를 제시함으로써
(B) 최근 연구 결과의 예를 제시함으로써

정답 (B)

해설 교수는 UCLA 연구에서 다룬 사례들과 그 결과를 설명하고 있다.

ORGANIZATION

(a) → (d) → (b) → (c)

Check-up for Vocabulary

1. safety concern 안전(에 대한) 염려
2. a violent quarrel 폭력 싸움
3. imitate an author's style 작가의 문체를 모방하다
4. confirm a reservation 예약을 확인하다
5. demonstrate the new theory 새로운 이론을 설명하다
6. a genuine Michelangelo's drawing 미켈란젤로의 진품

Skill Check-up 2

다음을 듣고 물음에 답하시오.

🎧 스크립트

P　Let's review now Raphael, one of the three major artists of the High Renaissance. He was born in Urbino in 1483. Raphael first learned about painting from his father, Giovanni Santi, who was an artist of minor reputation. In 1499, he moved to Perugia in Umbria and met the highly regarded Perugino. Raphael spent four years with Perugino learning all that Perugino could teach him. At the end of the four years, in 1504, Raphael moved to Florence. There he studied the works of Michelangelo, Leonardo Da Vinci, and Fra Bartolommeo. He learned the methods by which he could play with light, shadow, the anatomy and dramatic representation.

교수　전성기 르네상스에 속한 세 명의 주요 화가 가운데 한 명인 라파엘에 대해 살펴봅시다. 그는 1483년 우르비노에서 출생했습니다. 라파엘은 화가로서의 명성이 미미했던 아버지 조바니 산티에게서 처음 그림을 배웠습니다. 1499년에 움브리아 소재 페루자로 옮긴 후에 그는 명성이 자자했던 페루지노를 만나게 되지요. 그는 페루지노 곁에서 4년 동안 그에게서 배울 수 있는 모든 것을 배우게 됩니다. 4년이 지난 1504년에 라파엘은 플로렌스로 옮겨갑니다. 그 곳에서 그는 미켈란젤로, 레오나르도 다 빈치, 프라 바톨로메오 등의 작품을 연구하게 됩니다. 그리고 빛, 그림자, 해부, 극적인 묘사를 사용할 수 있는 방법에 대해 터득을 했습니다.

교수는 학생들에게 라파엘에 대해 어떻게 설명하는가?
(A) 출생 때부터의 그의 삶의 역사를 제공함으로써
(B) 그가 속한 시대의 중요 인물들을 나열함으로써

정답 (A)

해설　교수는 라파엘의 출생부터 시기별로 삶의 중요한 과정을 쫓아가며 그의 인생의 행로를 서술하고 있다.

ORGANIZATION

(b) → (e) → (a) → (c) → (d)

Check-up for Vocabulary

1. major cities 주요 도시들
2. born in to a rich family 부유한 가정에서 태어나
3. have a good reputation 좋은 평판을 가지고 있다
4. the highly educated 고등 교육을 받은 사람들

Skill Check-up 3

다음을 듣고 물음에 답하시오.

🎧 스크립트

P　As one of the major results of air pollution, acid rain is proving deadly to our environment.
S　How does air pollution become acid rain?
P　In some cases, acid rain is caused when industrial fumes mix with moisture in the atmosphere and become part of our rain fall. Another significant cause is automobile exhaust. Research has shown that sulfur dioxide from oil and nitrogen oxides produced from automobile engines have greatly intensified the problem.
S　Maybe electric cars would help reduce the acid rain then?
P　Actually they would still create problems. Recent studies show that electric power plants release more than 20 million tons of sulfur dioxide each year.

교수　대기 오염이 만들어내는 주요 결과물 중 하나인 산성비는 우리의 환경에 치명적이라는 점이 입증되고 있습니다.
학생　대기 오염이 어떻게 산성비가 되나요?
교수　몇몇 경우 산성비는 산업 가스가 대기 중의 수분과 혼합되다가 비에 섞여 내리지요. 또 다른 중대 원인은 자동차 배기 가스입니다. 연구결과에 따르면 기름에서 나오는 이산화물

과 자동차 엔진에서 배출되는 질산화물에서 발생하는 산화
물이 이 문제를 크게 악화시켰다고 합니다.

학생 그렇다면 전기 자동차를 사용할 경우 산성비를 감소시키는
데 도움이 될까요?

교수 사실 전기 자동차 또한 여전히 문제를 일으킵니다. 최근 연
구 결과에 따르면 전력 발전소에서도 매년 2천만 톤 이상의
이산화황을 배출한다고 합니다.

**교수는 산성비가 공기 오염의 결과라는 점을 어떤 방식으로 설명하
는가?**

(A) 산성비의 예들을 제시함으로써
(B) 산성비가 생성되는 방식을 설명함으로써

정답 (B)

해설 산업가스나 자동차 배기 가스가 대기 오염을 일으키는데, 산성비는
이런 오염 물질이 공기 중의 수분과 결합하여 생기는 것임을 설명하
고 있다.

Word Preview

☐ **fumes** (유해한) 연기, 연무   ☐ **intensify** 세게 하다, 강렬하게 만들다
☐ **exhaust** 배기가스   ☐ **electric power plant** 전력 발전소

ORGANIZATION
(c) → (d) → (b) → (e) → (a)

Check-up for Vocabulary
1. reduce risk 위험을 줄이다
2. industrial waste 산업 폐기물
3. automobile accidents 자동차 사고
4. intensify pressure 압력을 세게 하다
5. a siginificant event 중요한 행사
6. release the author's new book 작가의 신작을 발표하다

Skill Check-up 4

다음을 듣고 물음에 답하시오.

🎧 스크립트

S I'm taking on another class and I'm trying to decide on the best choice, Artifact Restoration or Anthropology.

P What is it you want to achieve with your degree?

S I'm hoping to work for a museum when I graduate.

P Ah! Then, my class is definitely the best choice for you. Anthropology is general and theoretical, whereas this class is highly specific and practical. You'll learn the skills you need through lectures and work

experience in actual museums.

S Sounds good, but doesn't it involve a lot more work?

P Actually no! Because it's a practical course there are no essays or exams. We evaluate you progressively through your work for the museums. It's simply a matter of pass or fail.

학생 수업을 하나 더 들으려고 하는데요. 유물 복원이나 인류학
중에서 선택하려 합니다.

교수 학위를 받고 나서 하고 싶은 것이 무엇인가?

학생 졸업하면 박물관에서 일하고 싶습니다.

교수 아! 그렇다면 내 수업이 자네에게 단연코 최선의 선택일 걸세.
인류학은 일반적이고 이론적이지만, 이 수업은 상당히 구체
적이고 실용적이거든. 자네는 강의나 실제 박물관에서의 실
습을 통해서 자네한테 필요한 기술을 익히게 된다네.

학생 멋진데요. 하지만 학습량이 훨씬 더 많지 않을까요?

교수 실제로는 그렇지 않아! 실용적인 과목이기 때문에 리포트를
쓸 일도 시험을 볼 일도 없으니까 말이야. 자네에 대한 평가
는 박물관에서 하는 일을 보면서 누진적으로 이루어지기 때
문에 단순히 통과나 낙제냐를 결정할 뿐이라네.

교수는 학생에게 어떤 방식으로 도움을 주는가?

(A) 두 가지 수업을 비교함으로써
(B) 자기 수업의 장점과 단점을 열거함으로써

정답 (A)

해설 교수는 학생의 학업 성취 목적을 듣고, 두 가지 수업의 성격을 비교하
면서 학생의 필요에 맞는 수업을 추천한다.

Word Preview

☐ **artifact** [고고학] 인공 유물   ☐ **restoration** 복원 (작업)
☐ **anthropology** 인류학

ORGANIZATION
(d) → (c) → (b) → (a)

Check-up for Vocabulary
1. achieve victory 승리를 거두다
2. practical English 실용 영어
3. the general public 일반 대중
4. get a high degree 높은 점수를 얻다
5. specific needs 특정 목표
6. evaluate the quality of the work 업무 성적을 평가하다

Exercise

■ Exercise 1

음악 수업의 강의를 듣고 물음에 답하시오.

🎧스크립트

P   What are two differences between Renaissance music and the 17th century style of music called Baroque? Does anyone know? It seems not, so I'll tell you. But, first, what is Baroque? The word Baroque comes from the Portuguese noun 'barroco' which means 'a pearl of irregular shape.' The modern use of the word Baroque is to describe the culture of that period, a culture which was highly expressive, confident and brilliant. Now the differences are the use of instruments and the introduction of soloists. Baroque uses instruments to produce music. This music complements but does not copy what the singer is doing with their voice. In the case of the Renaissance, if instruments were used at all they simply copied the singer's sound. The other difference, already mentioned, was the introduction of solos. In the Renaissance period, all sacred music was performed by choirs. In the Baroque period, soloists were used.

교수   르네상스 음악과 바로크라 불리는 17세기 음악의 두 가지 차이는 무엇일까요? 누구 아는 사람 있나요? 없는 것 같으니 제가 말해보죠. 그런데 먼저, 바로크란 무엇일까요? 바로크라는 단어는 포르투갈 어 명사인 '바로코'에서 유래되었습니다. 이는 '일그러진 진주'라는 뜻인데요. 현대에서 사용하는 바로크라는 단어는 그 당시의 문화, 즉 아주 표현이 풍부하고 자신만만하고 화려한 문화를 묘사하기 위해 사용되고 있습니다. 자, 그럼 차이점으로 가보죠. 그것은 악기의 사용과 독창자의 도입에 있습니다. 바로크 뮤직은 악기를 사용해서 음악을 만들어냅니다. 이 음악은 가수가 소리 내어 부르는 노래를 보완하는 것이지 흉내내는 것이 아닙니다. 르네상스 음악의 경우에는, 혹여 악기가 사용된다 하더라도 그저 가수의 소리를 단순하게 모방했을 뿐입니다. 앞서 언급했듯이 또 다른 차이점은 독창자의 도입입니다. 르네상스 시대에는 합창단이 모든 성가를 불렀습니다만, 바로크 시대에는 독창자가 사용되었습니다.

---

1 교수는 어떤 방식으로 바로크 음악을 소개하는가?
(A) 바로크라는 단어의 뜻을 설명함으로써
(B) 바로크 음악에 대해 몇 가지 질문을 던짐으로써
(C) 바로크 음악의 몇 가지 예를 제시함으로써
(D) 바로크 음악에 대해 다른 점을 설명함으로써

정답 (A)

해설   바로크 음악의 어원과 그 의미를 설명하고 현대적 의미를 제시함으로써 바로크 음악을 소개하였다.

2 교수에 따르면, 르네상스 음악과 바로크 음악의 차이점 두 가지는 무엇인가? 정답 두 개를 고르시오.
(A) 악기가 사용되는 방식
(B) 가수의 수
(C) 가수가 사용되는 방식
(D) 단어의 기원

정답 (A) (C)

해설   바로크 음악에서 악기의 역할은 가수의 목소리를 보완하지만 흉내내지 않는 반면, 르네상스 음악은 가수의 목소리를 단순히 흉내낸다. 또한 바로크 음악에서는 독창자를 사용하는 반면에 르네상스 음악에서는 모든 곡을 합창단이 부른다.

ORGANIZATION
produce music,
used,
copy the singer's sound,
not used

■ Exercise 2

건축학 수업의 강의를 듣고 물음에 답하시오.

🎧스크립트

P   Today we are going to study Gothic architecture. Let's begin by looking at some of its differences to Romanesque styles of architecture, which we studied last class. Romanesque architecture is designed more for protective purposes than for any artistic sense. The walls of Romanesque cathedrals are built thick to resist attacks by invaders. Gothic, on the other hand, has thinner walls, focusing more on art than function. You may remember that due to the thickness of the walls Romanesque cathedrals have very few windows. To brighten these cathedrals, they often add wall paintings and mosaics. Whereas Gothic makes great use of many stained glass windows to spread colored lighting creating a peaceful interior. Obviously these styles had very different purposes when built.

교수 오늘 우리는 고딕 건축에 대해 공부할 겁니다. 지난 수업 시간에 공부했던 로마네스크 건축 양식과의 몇 가지 차이점을 살펴보는 것으로 수업을 시작해 봅시다. 로마네스크 건축은 예술적인 감각보다는 방어를 목적으로 설계되었습니다. 로마네스크 양식으로 된 대성당의 벽은 침략자의 공격에 저항하기 위해 두껍게 만들어졌지요. 반면에 고딕 양식은 기능보다는 좀 더 예술적인 측면에 초점을 맞추었기 때문에 벽이 더 얇습니다. 벽의 두께 때문에 로마네스크 대성당에는 창문이 거의 없었다는 사실을 기억할 겁니다. 이런 대성당을 밝게 만들기 위해 사람들은 종종 벽화나 모자이크를 덧붙였습니다. 반면에 고딕 양식은 채색된 빛을 퍼지게 해서 평화로운 내부를 만들려고 스테인드 글라스를 많이 활용했습니다. 이 두 가지 스타일은 지을 당시 그 목적이 분명하게 매우 달랐습니다.

1 교수는 어떤 방식으로 고딕 건축에 대해 설명하는가?

(A) 고딕 건축의 역사적 배경을 설명함으로써
(B) 고딕 양식으로 지어진 건물을 슬라이드로 보여줌으로써
(C) 몇 가지 유명한 고딕 양식에 관한 이론을 제시함으로써
(D) 로마네스크 건축과 비교함으로써

정답(D)

해설 교수는 지난 수업 시간에 배웠던 로마네스크 양식과 고딕 양식이 서로 다른 목적을 가졌다고 말한다. 실용적 측면과 예술적 측면이라는 서로 다른 목적에 따라 두 건축 양식이 어떻게 달려졌는지 설명한다.

2 다음 중 두 가지 유형의 건축에 대해 언급하지 않은 것은?

(A) 창문의 숫자
(B) 벽의 목적
(C) 건물의 목적
(D) 건물로 빛이 들어오지 못하게 하는 방법

정답 (D)

해설 로마네스크 양식의 경우, 건물로 빛이 들어오지 못하게 한 것이 아니라 침략에 대비해서 벽을 두껍게 만들다 보니까 창문을 많이 설치할 수가 없었다.

ORGANIZATION

thin,
many,
resist attacks,
thick,
few

■ Exercise**3**

의학 수업의 강의를 듣고 물음에 답하시오.

🎧 스크립트

P Now we move on to the nervous system. To make it easier for you to memorize, let's split it into its two parts; the central nervous system and the peripheral nervous system. Use the initials CNS and PNS in your notes. Think of the latter as the information provider and the former as the information processor. The PNS communicates information, and the CNS decides what to do as a result of the information received. The CNS consists of the brain and the spinal cord. It's responsible for integrating, processing, and coordinating sensory data and motor commands. The CNS is also the seat of higher learning, performing such functions as intelligence, memory, learning, and emotion. The PNS includes all the neural tissue outside the CNS. The PNS carries motor commands to the peripheral tissues and systems.

교수 이제 신경계에 대해 알아봅시다. 여러분이 좀 더 쉽게 기억할 수 있게 하기 위해서, 이를 중추 신경과 말초 신경의 두 부분으로 나누어 봅시다. 여러분의 노트에는 CNS, PNS 라는 약자를 사용하세요. 후자(PNS)를 정보 제공자로 생각하고, 전자(CNS)를 정보 처리자로 생각합니다. PNS는 정보를 전달하고 CNS는 이 정보를 받아서 무엇을 할지 판단합니다. CNS는 두뇌와 척수로 이루어졌습니다. CNS는 감각 자료와 운동신경 명령을 통합하고, 처리하고, 조정하는 역할을 합니다. 또한 CNS는 좀더 상위의 고등 학습이 이루어지는 장소로 지능, 기억, 학습, 감정 등과 같은 기능을 수행합니다. PNS는 CNS 외의 모든 신경 조직을 포함합니다. PNS는 말초 조직과 체계에 운동 명령을 전달합니다.

1 교수는 어떤 방식으로 신경계를 설명하는가?

(A) 신경계를 두 부분으로 분류함으로써
(B) 신경계의 작용 과정을 설명함으로써
(C) 신체에 미치는 신경계의 영향을 논함으로써
(D) 신경계의 중요성을 강조함으로써

정답 (A)

해설 교수는 신경계를 중추 신경계(CNS)와 말초 신경계(PNS) 두 부분으로 나누어 비교 설명한다.

2 다음 중 사실이 아닌 것은? 정답 두 개를 고르시오.

(A) PNS가 CNS보다 더 지적이다.
(B) PNS가 CNS에 할 일을 말한다.
(C) PNS는 CNS로부터 지시를 받는다.
(D) PNS는 CNS를 위해 정보를 수집한다.

정답 (A) (B)

해설 CNS는 PNS에게서 정보를 받아 할 일을 지시하고, 좀 더 상위의 고등 학습을 한다.

ORGANIZATION

brain and spinal cord,
decide what to do,
neural tissue outside the CNS,
communicate information

■ Exercise 4

학생과 도서관 사서의 대화를 듣고 물음에 답하시오.

🎧 스크립트

S Ugh! Not again!

L Hey! Shush… remember it's a library!

S Sorry, it's just that's the third time I've tried downloading this file.

L What is it?

S A research paper. Every time I try, the download fails to complete.

L Have you tried refreshing the page, or using a mirror site?

S Yes, I tried both, but it still won't download.

L Hmmm… move over and let me try. Ah! I see the problem. The file's too large for this drive.

S Really? But it's a text document so it shouldn't be that large.

L Actually it is because it has a huge amount of high quality images which always take up a lot of space. You'd better use my work computer. Its main drive is larger.

학생 어머! 또야!

사서 학생, 조용히 해요. 여기가 도서관이란 사실을 명심해야죠.

학생 죄송합니다. 이 파일을 다운로드 받으려 한 게 벌써 세 번째 거든요.

사서 어떤 건데요?

학생 연구 논문이에요. 매번 다운로드를 시도할 때마다 실패하네요.

사서 페이지를 다시 열거나 미러 싸이트(인터넷 특정 사이트의 백업. 혼잡 회피를 위해 설치)를 사용해 봤어요?

학생 예, 두 가지 다 해봤어요. 하지만 여전히 다운로드가 되질 않아요.

사서 음… 옆으로 비켜 봐요. 내가 한번 해볼게요. 아! 무엇이 문제 인지 알겠군요. 이 드라이브에 담기에는 파일 용량이 너무 크네요.

학생 그래요? 하지만 이건 텍스트 문서라서 그렇게 클 리가 없는 데요.

사서 그건 아마도 공간을 많이 차지하는 고화질 이미지가 많아서 그럴 거에요. 제 작업용 컴퓨터를 사용해 보세요. 그건 메인 드라이브 용량이 더 크거든요.

---

1 남자는 어떤 방식으로 여자를 돕는가?

(A) 문제의 원인이 될만한 예를 지적함으로써
(B) 올바른 처리 과정을 보여줌으로써
(C) 그의 작업과 비교함으로써
(D) 컴퓨터의 서로 다른 기능을 강조함으로써

정답 (A)

해설 남자는 고화질 이미지가 용량을 많이 차지하기 때문에 다운로드가 쉽 지 않을 거라고 말한다.

2 남자가 자신의 컴퓨터를 사용하라고 권하는 이유는 무엇인가?

(A) 자신의 것이 최신 컴퓨터이기 때문에
(B) 여자가 사용하는 컴퓨터보다 드라이브 용량이 크기 때문에
(C) 여자가 사용하는 컴퓨터가 고장이기 때문에
(D) 여자가 사용하는 컴퓨터가 오프라인이기 때문에

정답 (B)

해설 여자가 다운 받으려는 자료에 공간을 많이 차지하는 고화질 이미지가 많아서 그녀가 사용하고 있는 컴퓨터 드라이브로는 다운로드를 받을 수 없다.

ORGANIZATION

Refreshing,
Mirror site,
images,
space,
A larger drive

Dictation for Exercise

Exercise 1 -------------------------------

① two differences between
② It seems not
③ which means
④ to describe the culture of that period
⑤ which was highly expressive
⑥ the use of
⑦ does not copy what the singer is doing
⑧ were used at all
⑨ already mentioned
⑩ was performed by choirs

✔Check-up for Expression

1. comes from
   모든 데이터는 메인 서버에서 나온다.

2. in the case of
   전송 에러인 경우에는 컴퓨터를 재부팅하는 것이 낫다.

3. performed by
   그의 부서에서는 거의 모든 작업을 로봇이 수행한다.

28

Exercise 2

① Let's begin by looking at
② for protective purposes
③ are built thick
④ has thinner walls
⑤ on art than function
⑥ they often add
⑦ to spread colored lighting
⑧ when built

✓ Check-up for Expression

1. Due to
   홍수 때문에 올해 농부들은 수확량이 적었다.
2. designed for
   이 트랙은 모형 자동차 레이스 용으로 설계되었다.
3. make use of
   네 자신의 경험을 이용하는 것이 아주 중요하다.

Exercise 3

① move on to
② To make it easier for you
③ let's split it into
④ Think of the latter
⑤ decides what to do
⑥ consists of
⑦ It's responsible for
⑧ is also the seat of
⑨ all the neural tissue outside

✓ Check-up for Expression

1. split into
   그 반은 그 문제로 인해 두 의견으로 갈라졌다.
2. responsible for
   그 보고서는 아이들의 폭력 증가가 대중 매체의 탓이라고 주장한다.
3. as a result of
   수요가 많아진 결과 그 제품 가격이 두 배로 올라갔다.

Exercise 4

① it's just that's the third time
② refreshing the page
③ it still won't
④ move over
⑤ it shouldn't be that large
⑥ take up a lot of space

✓ Check-up for Expression

1. take up
   그 회의는 생각보다 더 많은 공간을 차지할 것이다.
2. fails to
   그는 결코 사람의 이름을 잊는 적이 없다.
3. move over
   제 대신 이 책들 좀 옮겨 주세요.

Vocabulary Review

1. demonstrate	증명하다, 설명하다
2. link	유대, 관련
3. genuine	진짜의
4. imitate	모방하다
5. Gothic	고딕 양식의
6. confirm	확정[확인]하다
7. concern	염려, 걱정; 문제
8. refresh	[컴퓨터] (장치의 내용을) 재생하다
9. anatomy	해부(학)
10. invader	침략자, 침입자
11. major	주요한, (둘 중에서) 보다 많은
12. highly	높이, 크게
13. reputation	명성
14. fumes	(유해한) 연기, 연무
15. exhaust	배기가스
16. restoration	복원 (작업)
17. industrial	산업의
18. automobile	자동차
19. reduce	줄이다, 감소하다
20. release	내보내다, 방출하다
21. artifact	(고고학) 인공 유물
22. intensify	세게 하다, 강렬하게 만들다
23. anthropology	인류학
24. achieve	달성하다, 이루다
25. general	일반적인, 전반적인
26. degree	점수, 성적
27. specific	특정의; 구체적인
28. practical	실용적인, 실제의
29. evaluate	평가하다
30. irregular	불규칙한, 변칙적인
31. brilliant	훌륭한, 멋진
32. soloist	독주자, 독창자
33. complement	보완하다
34. protective	보호하는, 방어하는
35. take up	차지하다, 잡다
36. attack by ~	~에 의한 공격
37. born in ~	~에서 태어난
38. due to ~	~ 때문에, ~에 기인하는
39. make use of ~	~을 이용하다
40. move on to ~	~로 옮기다

CHAPTER 05

INFERENCE / STANCE

Sample

수학 수업의 토론을 듣고 물음에 답하시오.

교수 수학과 음악의 개념에 대해 생각할 때 여러분들은 둘 사이에 관련성이 있다고 생각되나요?

학생 아니요, 그다지 관련성은 없어 보입니다.

교수 대부분의 사람들이 그렇게 말합니다. 실제로 수학은 음악에 엄청난 영향을 미칩니다. 피타고라스는 음악을 위한 수학적 원리를 발견한 첫 인물입니다. 그는 현의 길이와 현이 진동하는 음조의 음높이 사이에 관련이 있다는 사실을 알아냈습니다.

학생 하지만 그것이 수학과 어떤 관련이 있습니까?

교수 피타고라스는 실험을 하다가 현이 짧을수록 음높이나 주파수가 더 높아진다는 사실을 발견했습니다. 그래서 현을 원래 길이의 반으로 줄이자 음조가 더 높아졌지요. 또한 현을 원래 길이의 반으로 줄이자 한 옥타브가 올라가고 그에 의해서 진동수가 두 배로 증가했다는 사실을 알아냈어요. 그게 바로 수학입니다!

교수의 다음 말이 의미하는 것은?

🎧 **That's what most people say.**

(A) 사람들은 수학이 음악에 커다란 영향을 미쳤다고 생각한다.
(B) 사람들은 수학이 실용적인 학문이라고 생각하지 않는다.
(C) 사람들은 수학과 음악 사이이 관련이 있다고 보지 않는다.
(D) 사람들은 수학이 음악 이론을 이해하는 데 아주 유용하다는 사실을 발견했다.

정답 (C)

해설 수학과 음악과의 관련성을 묻는 교수의 질문에 학생은 '관련성이 없는 것 같다'고 대답한다. 교수는 대부분의 사람들이 학생과 같은 생각을 하고 있다고 말하고 있다.

Skill Check-up

Skill Check-up : 1

다음을 듣고 물음에 답하시오.

🎧 스크립트

P In the 1400's, Portugal and Spain were in search of the ultimate prize of exploration – gold! Even though, from an historical perspective, the African slave trade seems racist, it was actually motivated by the economic benefits that it provided. The Spaniards needed cheap workers in America to work the mines to find the gold. Portugal got involved with this because they saw an opportunity to use these slaves as goods that they could trade with Spain. It should also be noted that some African nations themselves were only too willing to participate in the trade. The slaves' skin color or ethnic background was not that important. The focus was on the opportunity for economic enrichment.

교수 1400년 대에 포르투갈과 스페인은 탐험의 궁극적인 목적대상을 찾고 있었습니다. 바로 황금입니다. 역사적인 관점에서 본다면, 아프리카인 노예 무역이 인종차별주의적 행동 같지만, 실제로는 그것이 제공하는 경제적인 이익이 동기가 되었습니다. 스페인 사람들은 금을 찾기 위해 미국의 광산에서 일할 값싼 노동력이 필요했습니다. 포르투갈이 아프리카 노예 무역에 개입한 것은 이 노예들을 스페인과 교환할 수 있는 상품으로 사용할 기회를 포착했기 때문이었습니다. 여기서 언급하고 넘어가야 하는 사실은, 일부 아프리카 국가들도 이 무역에 기꺼이 참여하고자 했다는 것입니다. 노예들의 피부색이나 인종적 배경은 그다지 문제가 되지 않았습니다. 초점은 경제적인 풍족함을 이룰 기회를 포착했다는 것입니다.

강의를 통해 추론할 수 있는 것은?

(A) 일부 아프리카 국가들은 돈을 벌기 위해 자국 사람들을 거래했다.
(B) 아프리카인 노예 무역은 스페인과 포르투갈 사이의 정치적 투쟁을 유발시켰다.

정답 (A)

해설 최초의 아프리카 노예 무역은 현재 우리가 생각하는 것처럼 피부색이나 인종적 차별 때문이라기 보다 국가들 사이의 경제적 이익을 위해 생겨났다고 했다. 일부 아프리카 국가들이 노예 무역에 자발적으로 참여한 것도 돈을 벌기 위해서였다.

Word Preview

☐ **slave trade** 노예 무역
☐ **willing to** 기꺼이 ~하는
☐ **racist** 인종차별주의자의
☐ **enrichment** 풍부하게 함, 강화

ORGANIZATION

(d) → (a) → (b) → (c)

Check-up for Vocabulary

1. trade in furs 모피 무역
2. involve a lot of work 많은 일을 포함한다
3. equal opportunity 동등한 기회
4. participate in a debate 토론에 참여하다
5. ultimate goal in life 인생의 궁극적인 목표
6. motivate employees by rewarding them 보상을 통해 근로자들에게 동기를 부여하다

Skill Check-up 2

다음을 듣고 물음에 답하시오.

🎧 스크립트

P When people think of bacteria, they usually think of germs and disease. Most of us, however, tend to ignore the fact that there are literally thousands of bacteria that do good. One of the good things that bacteria does is decompose waste materials, and in the process, it helps to maintain nature's balance. Without these special bacteria, the remains of dead organisms and plants would not decay and pretty soon, there would be garbage everywhere! Actually, although bacteria can cause disease in humans, it can also help us to fight disease. For example, by injecting dead bacteria into the body, the body produces the same antibodies that it forms to protect itself against live bacteria. This process is called vaccination.

교수 사람들은 박테리아라면 주로 병원균이나 질병을 생각합니다. 그러나 우리들 대부분은 좋은 역할을 하는 박테리아도 그야말로 수 천 종류가 있다는 사실은 무시하는 경향이 있습니다. 박테리아가 주는 좋은 점 가운데 하나는 폐기물질을 분해하는 것입니다. 그리고 그 분해과정에서 자연의 균형을 유지하는 데 도움을 줍니다. 이런 특별한 박테리아가 없다면 죽은 유기체와 식물의 잔해가 썩지 않아 곧 사방이 쓰레기장이 될 겁니다. 물론, 실제로 박테리아가 인간에게 질병을 일으키기도 하지만, 또한 질병과 싸우는 데도 도움을 줍니다. 예를 들어, 우리 몸에 죽은 박테리아를 주입하면 이것이 살아 있는 박테리아에 대항할 똑같은 항체를 생산하지요. 이 과정을 백신접종이라고 합니다.

박테리아에 대한 교수의 태도는 어떤가?
(A) 박테리아는 나쁜 영향을 많이 끼친다고 생각한다.
(B) 박테리아는 여러 가지 면에서 유용하게 쓰일 수 있다고 지적한다.

정답 (B)

해설 박테리아는 폐기 물질을 분해하여 자연의 균형을 유지시켜주고, 질병에 대한 항체를 만들어내는 데 도움이 되는 등 유익한 경우가 많다.

Word Preview

☐ **germ** 세균, 병원균
☐ **decompose** 분해시키다
☐ **organism** 유기체, 미생물
☐ **decay** 썩다, 부패하다
☐ **vaccination** 백신[예방] 접종

ORGANIZATION

(b) → (d) → (e) → (c) → (a)

Check-up for Vocabulary

1. maintain a good condition 좋은 건강 상태를 유지하다
2. an influenza germ 병원균
3. ignore their opinions 그들의 의견을 무시하다
4. inject medicine into a vein 혈관에 약을 주사하다
5. protect eyes from the sun 태양으로부터 눈을 보호하다
6. a balance of mind and body 몸과 마음의 균형

Skill Check-up 3

다음을 듣고 물음에 답하시오.

🎧 스크립트

P Government Funded Health Care is a health insurance plan provided by the government that would give health insurance coverage to all people without discrimination. What do you think about this?

S1 I think poor people would like it but rich people would not.

P You have a point. Numerous individuals in the United States can't get proper health care because of either a lack of money or not having a job that provides health insurance. Having such a plan would allow these people to get the care they needed. The question is whether or not the U.S. should collect more taxes.

S2 I think we have enough tax money to pay for the health care. I think they should provide more jobs instead.

교수 정부 기금의 의료 보험이란 정부가 제공하는 건강보험 계획으로, 차별 없이 모든 사람에게 건강 보험 서비스를 주는 제도입니다. 여기에 대해 어떻게 생각하나요?

학생1 가난한 사람들은 좋아하겠지만, 부유한 사람들은 그렇지 않을 거라 생각합니다.

교수 일리 있는 말입니다. 수많은 미국인들이 돈이 없어서, 혹은 다니는 직장에서 건강 보험을 제공하지 않기 때문에 적절한 의료 치료를 받지 못하고 있습니다. 이 계획을 시행할 경우 이런 사람들이 필요한 치료를 받을 수 있게 됩니다. 문제는 (이 계획을 위해) 미국인들이 더 많은 세금을 거둬야 하는가에 있습니다.

학생2 우리는 이미 건강 보험을 위한 세금을 충분히 내고 있다고 생각합니다. 제 생각에는 그것보다 그들에게 더 많은 일자리를 제공하는 것이 낫다고 봅니다.

학생의 다음 말이 의미하는 것은?

🎧 **I think we have enough tax money to pay for the health care.**
(A) 가난한 사람을 돕기 위해 세금을 더 낼 필요가 있다.
(B) 세금을 더 내게 하는 것은 공평하지 않다.

정답 (B)

해설 가난한 사람들을 위해 세금을 더 걷는 것 보다 그들에게 더 많은 일자리를 제공해 스스로 그 문제를 해결하도록 하는 것이 좋다고 했다.

Word Preview

☐ **fund** 자금을 제공하다 　　☐ **health insurance** 건강 보험
☐ **discrimination** 차별

ORGANIZATION

(a) → (c) → (d) → (b)

Check-up for Vocabulary

1. life insurance 생명 보험
2. lack of skill 기술 부족
3. a numerous army 대군
4. take a proper step 적절한 조처를 취하다
5. provide 24-hour service 24시간 서비스를 제공하다
6. impose a heavy tax 과중한 세금을 부여하다

Skill Check-up : 4

다음을 듣고 물음에 답하시오.

🎧 스크립트

S1 Hey there. Did you go to the last class?
S2 Yeah, why?
S1 Oh, I missed it and I don't know when and where the final exam is.
S2 Why did you miss the class?
S1 I had the flu. I was so sick I couldn't even study.
S2 Are you feeling better now?
S1 Yes, much better. Thanks.
S2 Well... the exam is in the main hall, but... actually... the professor said he was putting the exam off for a week, so don't worry too much.
S1 So... there's a week's delay. That's great! I'll have time to review for it!
S2 Yeah, me too. Want to be my study partner?
S1 Sure.

학생1 안녕, 너 지난번 수업에 갔었니?
학생2 응. 왜?

학생1 저, 난 수업에 빠졌거든. 학기말 시험이 언제 어디서 하는지 몰라서.
학생2 수업은 왜 빠졌니?
학생1 독감에 걸렸었어. 너무 아파서 공부도 할 수가 없었어.
학생2 지금은 좀 나아졌니?
학생1 응, 훨씬 좋아졌어. 고마워.
학생2 음, 시험은 대강당에서 치를 거지만, 사실 교수님께서 시험을 일주일 연기한다고 하셨어. 그러니까 너무 걱정하지 마.
학생1 그러니까, 일주일 연기된단 말이지. 정말 잘됐다! 복습을 할 시간이 생겼네.
학생2 응, 나도 그래. 우리 같이 공부할래?
학생1 좋아.

남자의 기분이 어떠하겠는가?
(A) 공부하지 못해서 걱정이다.
(B) 공부할 시간이 생겨서 마음이 놓인다.

정답 (B)

해설 남학생은 독감 때문에 수업도 빠지고, 아파서 시험 공부도 못했었다. 시험이 연기되었다는 소식에 공부 시간을 확보했다며 기뻐한다.

Word Preview

☐ **flu** 독감, 유행성 감기 　　☐ **put off** 연기하다, 미루다
☐ **delay** 지연, 연기

ORGANIZATION

(d) → (c) → (b) → (a) → (e)

Check-up for Vocabulary

1. review the lessons 수업을 복습하다
2. miss an opportunity 기회를 놓치다
3. because of a traffic delay 교통이 막혀서
4. put off an appointment 약속을 미루다

Exercise

■ Exercise 1

법학 수업의 토론을 듣고 물음에 답하시오.

🎧 스크립트

P In a trial, lawyers often use rhetoric. Rhetoric, you know, is persuasive speaking. They sometimes use information favorable to them to win the case. Often a jury will not decide a case based on evidence but on the rhetoric. What do you think?
S1 Guilt and innocence, getting to the truth, is not the issue these days. Rhetoric serves only one purpose: to obscure the truth. Honest lawyers wouldn't practice law that way.

S2 I'm sorry but I can't agree with you. The use of rhetoric is neither good nor bad. What matters is why you use this skill. If my client is innocent, but I don't have the evidence to prove it, then I'll twist the truth using rhetoric. If the result is good then it doesn't matter if the complete truth wasn't told.

교수 재판에서 변호사들은 종종 웅변술을 사용합니다. 알다시피, 웅변이란 설득력 있는 말입니다. 그들은 때로 재판에서 이기기 위해 정보를 자신들에게 유리하게 사용하기도 하지요. 배심원들은 종종 증거를 바탕으로 하지 않고 바로 이 말을 기준으로 사건 결정을 내리기도 합니다. 여러분의 생각은 어떤가요?

학생1 요즘은 유죄나 무죄같이 진실에 도달하는 것은 문제가 아닌 것 같아요. 웅변(수사학적 기교)은 단 한 가지 목적만을 충족시킵니다. 바로 진실을 덮는 겁니다. 정직한 변호사는 그런 식으로 변호하지 않습니다.

학생2 미안하지만 제 의견은 다릅니다. 웅변의 사용은 좋은 것도 나쁜 것도 아니고, 단지 이런 기술을 사용하는 이유가 무엇인가의 문제입니다. 만약 제 의뢰인이 무죄인데 그것을 입증할 증거가 없다면 저는 이 기술을 사용해서 진실을 왜곡할 수도 있습니다. 만약 결과가 좋다면 완벽한 진실을 말했는지 아닌지의 여부는 중요하지 않습니다.

1 웅변의 사용에 대한 여학생의 의견은 어떤가?
(A) 사용하면 안되는 나쁜 것이라 생각한다.
(B) 변호사가 웅변을 보다 더 많이 사용해야 한다고 생각한다.
(C) 좋은 목적으로 사용하는 것은 괜찮다고 생각한다.
(D) 변호사가 웅변을 사용하는 것은 정직하지 못하다고 생각한다.
정답 (C)

해설 여학생은 웅변 자체가 좋고 나쁜 것이 아니라, 그것을 사용하는 이유가 중요하다고 생각한다. 좋은 이유로 사용한다면 완벽하게 진실을 말했는지의 여부는 중요하지 않다.

2 교수의 말에 따르면, 웅변이란 무엇입니까?
(A) 정말 좋은 이야기를 말하는 능력
(B) 진리를 은폐하는 능력
(C) 사람을 납득시키는 능력
(D) 진리를 입증하는 능력
정답 (C)

해설 교수는 웅변을 설득력 있는 말이라 정의한다.

ORGANIZATION

persuasive speaking,
rhetoric,
A jury,
rhetoric,
evidence,
obscure the truth,
neither good nor bad

■ Exercise **2**

심리학 수업의 대화를 듣고 물음에 답하시오.

🎧 스크립트

P Today's lecture is on stress: what it is, what causes it, and how it can be cured. Stress affects everyone and everything. One way of describing stress is nervousness, anxiety, mental discomfort, or pressure. There are many things that cause stress. Any ideas?

S I sometimes find socializing stressful. *(Everyone laughs.)*

P Popularity, friends, relationships, and looks are often stressful for teenagers. However, adults tend to face different kinds of stress such as meeting business deadlines. But everybody is affected by stress when it comes to things like wars, pollution, or crime. It is important to learn how to live with these situations because it's nearly impossible to get through life without encountering them. Physicians have proved that diseases brought on by stress are more likely to happen to people with very busy lives.

S Let's all go home and take a nap then! *(More laughs.)*

교수 오늘 강의는 스트레스에 관해서입니다. 스트레스가 무엇인지, 스트레스의 원인이 무엇인지, 스트레스를 어떻게 치료할 수 있는지 등 말입니다. 스트레스는 모든 사람과 모든 것에 영향을 줍니다. 스트레스는 긴장, 불안, 정신적 불쾌감, 압박감 등으로 표현할 수 있습니다. 스트레스를 유발하는 원인은 많습니다. 어떤 것이 있을까요?

학생 저는 때로 사람들을 사귀는 게 스트레스가 되는 것 같아요. (모두 웃는다.)

교수 10대들에게는 종종 인기나 친구, 여러 관계들 또는 외모 같은 것들이 스트레스의 원인이 되고는 합니다. 그러나 성인들의 경우에는 업무 마감 날짜를 맞추는 것 같은 다른 종류의 스트레스를 받는 경향이 있습니다. 하지만 전쟁, 오염, 범죄와 같은 문제에 이르면 모든 사람이 스트레스의 영향을 받습니다. 이런 문제에 부닥치지 않고 살아가는 것은 거의 불가능하기 때문에 이런 상황과 더불어 사는 방법을 배우는 것이 중요합니다. 의사들은 스트레스에 의해 초래되는 질병이 아주 바쁘게 살아가는 사람에게서 발생할 가능성이 더욱 높다는 사실을 입증하기도 했지요.

학생 자, 모두들 집에 가서 낮잠이나 잡시다!(웃음소리가 커진다.)

1 교수가 다음과 같이 말할 때 그 의미는 무엇인가?

🎧 It is important to learn how to live with these situations because it's nearly impossible to get through life without encountering them.

(A) 스트레스는 우리들에게 매우 좋은 영향을 끼칠 수 있다.
(B) 의사들의 도움으로 스트레스를 피하기가 불가능하다.
(C) 스트레스는 이를 가진 사람 모두를 병들게 만든다.
(D) 스트레스는 우리가 더불어 사는 방법을 배워야만 하는 무엇이다.

정답 (D).

해설 스트레스에 직면하지 않고 살아가는 것은 거의 불가능하기 때문에 스트레스를 유발하는 상황과 더불어 살아가는 방법을 배워야 한다고 강조한다.

2 다음 중 스트레스의 원인으로 언급되지 않은 것은?

(A) 업무 마감 일자를 맞추는 것
(B) 오염이나 범죄 같은 사회 문제
(C) 친구 간의 관계
(D) 시험 성적에 대한 걱정

정답 (D)

ORGANIZATION

nervousness / anxiety / mental discomfort / pressure,
popularity / friends / relationships / looks,
meeting business deadlines,
wars / pollution / crime

■ Exercise3

생물학 수업의 대화를 듣고 물음에 답하시오.

🎧 스크립트

P Science has always been filled with controversy. For example, breakthroughs in areas such as artificial insemination have caused much debate in the past. However, time has proved that such advances are worthwhile. The same could happen with cloning. What do you think about this?

S Well... I always thought of it as good.

P Many people feel that way. But protesters who feel that cloning should be banned don't really understand it. In fact, many arguments against human cloning are misconceptions. One popular myth is that people think cloning technology can produce an exact copy of an existing human being. This is not true. Cloning technology can only produce a cloned embryo and the developed child would have unique experiences. People also think that a clone will be both behaviorally and physically identical to its donor. This also is not true.

교수 과학은 언제나 논쟁거리로 가득찼습니다. 예를 들어, 인공 수정과 같은 영역의 비약적인 발전은 과거에 많은 논쟁을 일으켰습니다. 그러나 시간이 흐르면서 이와 같은 진보가 가치 있었다는 점이 입증되고 있습니다. 클로닝(동식물의 한 개체에서 수정을 거치지 않고, 무성생식에 의하여 양친과 똑같은 유전자 조성을 가진 개체를 얻는 기술)이라는 영역에서도 동일한 일이 일어날 수 있겠죠. 여러분은 여기에 대해 어떻게 생각하나요?

학생 음… 저는 항상 좋은 것으로 생각했습니다.

교수 많은 사람들이 그렇게 느낍니다. 하지만 클로닝을 금지시켜야 한다고 느끼는 반대자들은 사실 제대로 이해하지 못하고 있습니다. 실제, 인간 복제를 둘러싼 많은 논쟁은 클로닝을 잘못 이해한 데서 비롯되었습니다. 한 가지 사회적 통념은 클로닝 기술을 사용하여 현재 생존해 있는 인간과 완전히 동일한 복제 인간을 생산해낼 수 있다고 생각하는 겁니다. 이것은 사실이 아닙니다. 클로닝 기술은 무성 생식된 태아를 생산할 수 있을 뿐이고, 이후 성장하는 아이는 자신만의 독자적인 경험을 하게 될 겁니다. 또한 사람들은, 클론이 행동적으로나 신체적으로 그 기증자와 동일하리라고 생각합니다. 이것 또한 사실이 아닙니다.

1 교수의 다음과 같은 말을 통해 추론할 수 있는 것은 무엇인가?

🎧 The same could happen with cloning.

(A) 언젠가 클로닝 분야에서 비약적인 발전이 있을지도 모른다.
(B) 언젠가 클로닝이 더 이상 가치 없어질 지도 모른다.
(C) 언젠가 클로닝이 좋은 일이라 입증될 지도 모른다.
(D) 언젠가 클로닝에 대해 더 이상의 논쟁이 없을 것이다.

정답 (C)

해설 인공 수정이 비약적으로 발전했을 때 많은 논쟁이 있었지만, 시간이 흐르면서 가치 있는 일로 입증된 것처럼 무성 생식 또한 후에 가치 있는 일로 입증 받을 가능성이 있다.

2 대화의 일부를 다시 한번 들으시오.

🎧 One popular myth is that people think cloning technology can produce an exact copy of an existing human being. This is not true.

교수가 다음과 같이 말할 때 그 말이 의미하는 것은 무엇인가?

🎧 This is not true.

(A) 대부분의 사람들은 클로닝을 좋아하지 않는다.
(B) 좀 더 많은 사람들이 클로닝을 인정할 필요가 있다.
(C) 일부 논쟁은 그릇된 생각을 바탕으로 한다.
(D) 대부분의 논쟁은 매우 대중적인 통념이다.

정답 (C)

ORGANIZATION

worthwhile,
an exact copy,
identical to its donor,
a cloned embryo

■ Exercise 4

두 학생의 대화를 듣고 물음에 답하시오.

🎧 스크립트

S1 Oh, man! This is so hard!
S2 What's wrong?
S1 I just can't figure out the essay.
S2 What's your topic?
S1 'How has fear become the source of power in modern American politics.'
S2 Really? You won't believe this, but just this morning our class watched an excellent BBC video that'd help you. It's about the US President and his use of fear. He pretends there's a global terror organization. We get very afraid, and so then we give him all the power he wants.
S1 Ah… I get it now. He scares us into giving him power in return for protection from things that doesn't exist. Just like those weapons of mass destruction that weren't really there. Hmmm… I wonder if your professor took that video home or left it in the classroom.

학생1 세상에! 이거 정말 힘들군!
학생2 뭐가 잘못 됐니?
학생1 이 보고서를 어떻게 써야 할지 모르겠어.
학생2 주제가 뭔데?
학생1 '공포가 어떻게 현대 미국 정치에서 권력의 출처가 되어가는가'야.
학생2 정말? 믿기 힘들겠지만, 나 바로 오늘 아침 수업시간에 너에게 도움이 될만한 훌륭한 BBC 비디오를 봤어. 미국 대통령과 그의 공포의 구사에 대한 내용이야. 그는 전세계적인 테러 조직이 존재한다고 가장해. 그러면 우리는 이에 대해 매우 두려워지는 거지. 그래서 그가 원하는 모든 권력을 그에게 부여하게 되는 거야.
학생1 아… 이제 알겠어. 그는 우리를 공포에 떨게 해서 존재하지 않는 것으로부터 보호 받는 대가로 자신에게 권력을 주게 한 거군. 실제로는 존재하지 않았던 대량 살상 무기처럼 말이야. 음… 네 교수님이 그 비디오를 댁에 가져가셨는지 아니면 교실에 남겨두셨는지 궁금하다.

1 대화의 일부를 다시 들으시오.

🎧 You won't believe this, but just this morning our class watched an excellent BBC video that'd help you.

여자가 다음과 같이 말할 때 그 의미는 무엇인가?

🎧 You won't believe this

(A) 남학생에게 도움이 될 정보를 자신이 가지고 있다는 점을 말하려고
(B) 그녀가 도와줄 수 있다는 사실을 남학생이 믿어야 한다고 말하려고
(C) 남학생이 처한 상황에 대해 안쓰럽게 생각한다는 점을 말하려고
(D) 자신도 보고서에 대해 걱정하고 있다는 점을 말하려고

정답 (A)

해설 그날 수업시간에 본 비디오가 남학생의 과제물 작성에 도움이 된다는 사실을 말해주려는 의도에서 한 말이다.

2 남자는 다음에 어떤 일을 하겠는가?

(A) 여자의 집을 방문할 것이다.
(B) 정보를 좀 더 찾기 위해 도서관에 갈 것이다.
(C) 자신의 교수에게 시간을 좀 더 달라고 할 것이다.
(D) 여학생의 교수에게 비디오에 대해 물어볼 것이다.

정답 (D)

해설 마지막 말을 보면, 남자는 여자가 언급한 비디오에 관심이 갔기 때문에 여자의 교수에게 비디오를 구하려 할 것이다.

ORGANIZATION

How has fear become the source of power in modern American politics,
BBC video,
US President and his use of fear,
a global terror organization

Dictation for Exercise

Exercise 1 ----------------------------------

① In a trial
② is persuasive speaking
③ favorable to them to win
④ based on evidence
⑤ to obscure the truth
⑥ wouldn't practice law
⑦ neither good nor bad
⑧ I'll twist the truth
⑨ wasn't told

Check-up for Expression

1. persuasive
   그 정치가는 아주 설득력 있는 대화술을 가지고 있다.
2. What matters is
   중요한 것은 이것이 질병을 치료하는 데 매우 효과적이냐는 것이다.
3. based on
   그의 말은 자신의 연구에 바탕한 것이다.

Exercise 2

① is on stress
② how it can be cured
③ find socializing stressful
④ tend to face
⑤ is affected by
⑥ when it comes to things like
⑦ nearly impossible to get through
⑧ have proved
⑨ brought on by stress
⑩ take a nap then

✔**Check-up for Expression**

1. is likely to
   오늘 오후에 비가 올 것 같다.
2. get through
   이 일을 끝내기 위해서 우리는 많은 어려움을 극복해야 했다.
3. tend to
   사람들은 자주 브랜드를 바꾸는 경향이 있다.

Exercise 3

① has always been filled with
② in areas such as
③ have caused much debate
④ The same could happen
⑤ thought of it as good
⑥ should be banned
⑦ an exact copy of
⑧ would have unique experiences
⑨ identical to its donor

✔**Check-up for Expression**

1. was filled with
   소녀의 마음은 놀람으로 가득찼다.
2. identical to
   이 스타일은 어느 것과도 같지 않고 독특합니다.
3. banned
   많은 사람들이 핵실험이 금지되어야 한다는 데 동의한다.

Exercise 4

① I just can't figure out
② the source of power
③ You won't believe this
④ that'd help you
⑤ He pretends
⑥ scares us into
⑦ in return for
⑧ I wonder if

✔**Check-up for Expression**

1. figure out
   무엇이 문제인지 알아냈니?
2. wonder if
   나는 그것이 이 계획에 좋은 아이디어인지 궁금하다.
3. in return for
   네가 도와준 것에 대해 어떻게 보상하면 좋겠니?

Vocabulary Review

1. germ — 세균, 병원균
2. slave trade — 노예 무역
3. jury — 배심(원단)
4. motivate — 동기를 부여하다, 자극을 주다
5. opportunity — 기회
6. decay — 썩다, 부패하다
7. vaccination — 백신[예방] 접종
8. guilt — 유죄, 범죄
9. organism — 유기체, 미생물
10. inject — 주사하다
11. fund — 자금을 제공하다
12. flu — 독감, 유행성 감기
13. delay — 지연, 연기
14. trial — 재판, 공판
15. maintain — 유지하다
16. obscure — 가리다, 은폐하다
17. enrichment — 풍부하게 함, 강화
18. ultimate — 궁극적인
19. trade — 무역
20. pretend — ~인 체하다, 가장하다
21. scare — 위협하다, 겁나게 하다
22. health insurance — 건강 보험
23. discrimination — 차별
24. breakthrough — (과학 등의) 큰 약진, 새로운 발견
25. protester — 항의하는 사람, 이의 제기자
26. ban — 금지하다, 반대하다
27. misconception — 잘못된 생각, 오해
28. face — 직면하다; 마주하다
29. racist — 인종차별주의자의
30. decompose — 분해시키다
31. wonder if ~ — ~인지 아닌지 모르다
32. willing to ~ — 기꺼이 ~하는

33. participate in ~	~에 참여하다
34. put off	연기하다, 미루다
35. tend to ~	~하는 경향이 있다
36. get through ~	~을 극복하다, 끝내다
37. be likely to ~	~할 것 같다
38. identical to ~	~와 꼭 같은, 일치하는
39. figure out	이해하다; 해결하다
40. in return for ~	~의 답례로, ~의 회답으로

CHAPTER 06
FUNCTION

Sample

심리학 수업의 대화를 듣고 물음에 답하시오.

교수 스키너의 전체 이론은 작동적 조건 형성(시행 착오적 학습)에 기초합니다. 유기체는 자신의 행동을 더 강화하거나 약화시키는 자극에 마주칠 때까지 이리 저리 다닙니다. 이 자극이라는 것은 막 발생했던 행동을 증가시키거나 약화시키는 효과가 있습니다. 이것이 작동적 조건 형성입니다. 즉 행동에는 결과가 따르고 그 결과는 유기체의 미래의 행동에 영향을 미칩니다. 이해가 되었나요?

학생 음, 글쎄요. 그런 것 같지 않습니다.

교수 그렇다면, 좋아요. 한 쪽 벽에 페달이 있는 특별한 우리에 쥐가 들어 있다고 상상해 봅시다. 페달을 누르면 우리 안으로 작은 알갱이 같은 먹이가 나오는 거예요. 쥐는 평상시와 같이 우리 안에서 이리저리 다니다가, 우연히 페달을 누르게 되는 거죠. 그러면 마치 마술처럼 작은 알갱이 같은 먹이가 우리 안으로 떨어지는 겁니다. 바로 그때 쥐는 더 많은 음식을 얻기 위해 맹렬하게 페달을 밟아 댈 겁니다.

교수가 우리 안의 쥐를 언급한 이유는 무엇인가?
(A) 작동적 조건 형성에 대한 예를 들기 위해
(B) 실험 아이디어를 제안하기 위해
(C) 쥐가 우리에 갇혔을 때 어떤 행동을 하는지 보여주기 위해
(D) 작동적 조건 형성 실험에서의 쥐의 특별한 역할을 설명하기 위해

정답 (A)

해설 학생이 작동적 조건 형성에 대한 설명을 제대로 이해하지 못하자, 교수는 학생의 이해를 돕기 위해 그 같은 사례를 다룬 한 실험을 예로 들고 있다.

Skill Check-up

Skill Check-up : 1

다음을 듣고 물음에 답하시오.

 스크립트

S Excuse me, Professor. I'm having some trouble with my experiment. Could you advise me?

P What seems to be the problem?

S Well, I'm having a few problems with my pilot questionnaire. People are misunderstanding some of the instructions and filling them in wrong.

P So... what's the problem? *(Thinking it is going well.)*

S Well, I... I thought I just told you. People are filling them in wrong.

P Well, that's the whole point of conducting a pilot study – to find out what works and what doesn't work before you give the questionnaire to more people. If there are problems, you should fix them before doing the final questionnaire. Do you need help to correct these problems?

S Oh, I see… no, it's okay, I can do that. Thanks, Professor.

학생 교수님, 실례합니다. 제가 하고 있는 실험에 어려움이 좀 있어서요. 조언을 좀 해주시겠어요?

교수 문제가 무엇인가?

학생 음, 예비 설문지에 몇 가지 문제점이 있습니다. 사람들이 몇몇 지시사항들을 제대로 이해하지 못해서 잘못된 답을 기입하거든요.

교수 그런데… 그게 무슨 문제가 되지? (잘 진행되고 있다고 생각하면서.)

학생 글쎄요. 제가… 방금 말씀 드렸는데요. 사람들이 설문지를 잘못 기입합니다.

교수 음… 그것이 바로 예비 조사를 수행하는 전체 핵심이네. (예비 조사라는 것이) 좀 더 많은 사람에게 설문지를 돌리기 전에 어떤 것이 제대로 되고 어떤 것이 제대로 안 되는지를 알아보는 거란 말이지. 문제가 있다면 최종 설문지를 만들기 전에 고치면 되는 거야. 학생이 그런 문제를 수정하는 데 도움이 필요한 건가?

학생 아, 알겠습니다. 아니요, 괜찮습니다. 제가 할 수 있습니다. 감사합니다, 교수님.

교수가 다음과 같이 말하는 이유는 무엇인가?

🎧 So... what's the problem?

(A) 아무런 문제가 없다고 생각한다는 것을 나타내려고
(B) 학생이 말하는 문제가 무엇인지 이해하지 못했음을 나타내려고

정답 (A)

해설 교수는 학생이 지금 겪고 있는 문제는 예비 조사에서 있을 수 있는 정상적인 현상이므로 전혀 문제될 것이 없다고 말하고 있다.

Word Preview

- □ **pilot** 시험적인, 예비의
- □ **conduct** (업무 등을) 수행[처리]하다
- □ **questionnaire** 앙케이트, 질문서

ORGANIZATION

(c) → (a) → (b) → (d)

Check-up for Vocabulary

1. fix a machine 기계를 수리하다
2. correct errors 오류를 정정하다
3. a pilot study 실험적 연구
4. a chemical experiment 화학 실험
5. conduct a questionnaire 설문조사를 실시하다
6. follow the instructions 사용설명서를 따르다

Skill Check-up 2

다음을 듣고 물음에 답하시오.

🎧 스크립트

P Our rain forests are being destroyed at an alarming rate. Even though there are no rain forests in most countries, still rain forests greatly affect all of us around the world. Rain forests are the home of about fifty percent of all species. It's also a vital health resource so they must be protected for the good of all people. Many medicines are found in the rain forests which treat common diseases. You know what malaria is, right? It's a disease that is treated with quinine, which is taken from the cinchona tree in Peru.

교수 우리의 열대 우림이 우려될만한 속도로 파괴되고 있습니다. 대부분의 국가에 열대 우림이 없기는 하지만, 열대 우림은 여전히 전 세계의 우리 모두에게 지대한 영향을 미칩니다. 열대 우림은 모든 (생물) 종의 약 50%가 속한 집입니다. 또한 필수적인 건강 자원이기도 하지요. 그래서 모든 사람의 이익을 위해 보호되어야 합니다. 흔한 질병을 치료하는 여러 많은

약이 열대 우림에서 발견됩니다. 여러분들 말라리아가 무엇인지 알죠? 말라리아는 키니네 제를 가지고 치료되는 질병인데 이 키니네는 페루에 있는 기나피 제제에서 추출됩니다.

교수가 말라리아에 대한 언급한 이유는 무엇인가?

(A) 열대 우림에서 찾은 약으로 고칠 수 있는 병의 예를 들려고
(B) 열대 우림에 일부 질병의 원인이 되는 식물들이 있음을 지적하려고

정답 (A)

해설 교수는 열대 우림이 필수적인 건강 자원이기 때문에 인류에게 중요하다고 설명하면서, 말라리아를 예로 든다. 열대 우림의 식물에서 말라리아의 치료제가 추출된다.

Word Preview

- □ **rain forest** 열대 우림
- □ **resource** 자원, 재원
- □ **species** (생물) 종

ORGANIZATION

(c) → (d) → (b) → (a)

Check-up for Vocabulary

1. liquid medicine 물약
2. a natural resource 천연 자원
3. a tropical rain forest 열대 우림 지역
4. endangered species 멸종 위기의 종들
5. destroy the building 건물을 파괴하다
6. a common language 공용어

Skill Check-up 3

다음을 듣고 물음에 답하시오.

🎧 스크립트

P I think you'll agree that scientific discoveries are becoming increasingly impressive. A variety of pills are now readily available by prescription that can alter one's mind or personality. However, there is a strong moral dilemma over whether these pills should be taken and accepted. Opinions?

S1 Man-made substances that alter personality change a person. I believe that only certain types of illnesses, a mental disease, should warrant such medicines, and only temporarily.

S2 I think it is hard to make a judgment on whether someone should take such medicine. No one is truly capable of deciding what degree of severity another person is at. Well, who is normal, and who is abnormal?

교수	과학적인 발견이 점점 강한 인상을 남긴다는 데 여러분 모두 동의하리라 생각합니다. 이제는 약 처방만 있으면 사람의 마음이나 성격을 변화시킬 수 있는 다양한 약을 입수할 수 있게 되었습니다. 그러나, 거기에는 이런 약을 인정하고 복용해도 되는지에 대한 격렬한 윤리적 딜레마가 있습니다. 누가 이에 대해 말해보겠습니까?
학생1	성격을 바꾸는 합성 물질은 사람을 바꿉니다. 저는, 단지 일정 형태의 질병, 말하자면 정신질환에만 이런 약을, 그것도 일시적으로만 허가해야 한다고 생각합니다.
학생2	누가 약을 먹어야 하는지 판단을 내리기는 아주 어려울 것 같습니다. 그 누구도 어떤 사람이 어느 정도의 고통을 받고 있는지 가늠할 수 없어요. 그러니까... 어떤 사람이 정상인 걸까요. 그리고 어떤 사람이 비정상인 거죠?

남자가 다음과 같이 말하는 이유는 무엇인가?

🎧 Well, who is normal? And Who is abnormal?

(A) '정상'과 '비정상'의 차이를 물어보기 위해
(B) 여학생의 의견에 반박하기 위해

정답 (B)

해설 남자는 사람의 정신과 성격에 영향을 미치는 약은 한정된 사람들에게 일시적으로만 허용해야 한다는 여자의 의견을, 그 기준자체를 정하기가 어렵다는 이야기를 통해 반박한다.

Word Preview

☐ **prescription** 처방(약)　　☐ **alter** 바꾸다, 변경하다
☐ **abnormal** 비정상의, 예외의

ORGANIZATION

(e) → (b) → (a) → (c) → (d)

Check-up for Vocabulary

1. alter a policy 정책을 바꾸다
2. warrant quality 품질을 보증하다
3. available for rent 임대가 가능한
4. scientific research 과학적 연구
5. abnormal behavior 비정상적인 행동
6. get over the dilemma 딜레마를 극복하다

Skill Check-up 4

다음을 듣고 물음에 답하시오.

🎧 스크립트

S	Hi. I was wondering about the possibility of graduating early. I have a job opportunity that I'd like to take but I need to graduate first.
C	Well, it's not common, but some students can graduate early. What it takes is a grade average in the top five percent, special circumstances, and a signed agreement from all of your lecturers.
S	My grades have been good this term, and I'm very committed to achieving my ambitions.
C	That's all good and well, but... I see that you've missed two deadlines this semester. If you want to graduate early, you must keep all of your deadlines in the future.
S	Okay. I will.
C	You should submit your application for early graduation to student administration, only when you keep the rest of the deadlines.

학생	안녕하세요? 조기 졸업을 할 수 있는 가능성에 대해 알고 싶어서요. 취직 기회가 와서 수락하고 싶은데 우선 졸업을 해야 하거든요.
상담자	음, 흔한 일은 아니지만, 일찍 졸업할 수 있는 경우도 있어요. 필요 조건은 평균 학점이 상위 5퍼센트에 속하고, 특별한 상황에 있는 경우, 또는 강의하는 교수님 모두가 서명날인한 동의서를 갖추어야 해요.
학생	이번 학기에는 학점이 좋아요. 그리고 포부를 이루려고 열심히 노력했어요.
상담자	아주 좋아요. 하지만 학생은 이번 학기에 이미 제출 마감 기한을 두 번 놓쳤군요. 조기 졸업을 하고 싶으면 앞으로 있을 마감 기한을 전부 지켜야만 해요.
학생	예, 알겠습니다.
상담자	나머지 마감 기한을 다 지킨 경우에 한해서만 조기 졸업 신청서를 학생 총무처에 제출하도록 하세요.

남자가 다음과 같이 말하는 이유는 무엇인가?

🎧 You should submit your application for early graduation to student administration, only when you keep the rest of the deadlines.

(A) 여학생이 조기 졸업할 자격을 갖추지 못했다는 사실을 지적하려고
(B) 마감 기한을 지키는 것이 중요하다는 것을 강조하려고

정답 (B)

해설 조기 졸업의 전제 조건은 앞으로의 마감 기한을 모두 지키는 것이다.

Word Preview

☐ **early graduation** 조기 졸업　　☐ **application** 신청서

ORGANIZATION

(a) → (c) → (b) → (e) → (d)

Check-up for Vocabulary

1. sign our names 서명하다
2. submit a resume 이력서를 제출하다
3. achieve success 성공을 이루다
4. meet the deadline 마감 기한을 지키다
5. graduate from Oxford 옥스포드를 졸업하다
6. fill out an application 신청서를 작성하다

Exercise

■ Exercise 1

고대 역사 수업의 강의를 듣고 물음에 답하시오.

🎧 스크립트

P A mummy is a preserved body. Egyptians believed that every person had a soul that would live on after death and if the person's body was destroyed, the spirit might not be able to survive. To properly preserve the body for the passage into the afterlife, it would have to be mummified. The Egyptian body preservation process was a complicated procedure performed by priests. They took out the brain and most of the internal organs, stuffing the empty insides with sawdust or linen pads. Then they filled the body with an embalming fluid. Finally, they wrapped the mummy in cloth and placed it in a coffin that was shaped like a human. Egyptians that were mummified were normally the most important in society, so they had many of their riches or treasures buried with them.

교수 미라는 보존된 시체입니다. 이집트 사람들은 모든 사람에게는 영혼이 있어서 죽은 후에도 계속 살게 된다고 믿었습니다. 그래서 인간의 신체가 파괴되면 그 영혼이 살 수 없을지도 모른다고 생각했지요. 때문에 인간의 몸을 완전하게 보존하여 내세로 보내기 위해서는 시체를 미라로 만들어야 했습니다. 이집트의 시체 보존 과정은 성직자에 의해 시행되는 복잡한 과정이었습니다. 그들은 뇌와 대부분의 장기를 꺼내고 빈 내부를 톱밥이나 리넨(천의 일종) 패드로 채웠습니다. 그런 다음 시체에 방부제를 채웠습니다. 마지막으로, 천으로 미라를 싼 후에 인간의 모양을 한 관에 넣었습니다. 미라로 만들어진 이집트인들은 보통 사회에서 매우 중요한 인물이었습니다. 그래서 그들이 가진 많은 재산이나 보물을 그들과 함께 묻었습니다.

1 교수가 인간의 영혼에 대해 언급한 이유는 무엇인가?

(A) 이집트인들이 내세를 믿었다는 것을 강조하려고
(B) 잘 만들어진 미라의 예를 들려고
(C) 이집트인들이 미라를 만든 이유를 제시하려고
(D) 영혼을 가진 시체를 보존하는 일이 어렵다는 것을 설명하려고

정답 (C)

해설 이집트 인들은 인간이 영혼을 가지고 있기 때문에 죽은 후에도 계속 살 수 있을 거라고 믿었다. 때문에 내세에서의 삶을 위해 시체를 손상시키지 않고 보존할 필요가 있었던 것이다.

2 다음 중 미라를 만드는 과정이 아닌 것은?

(A) 관에 심장을 넣는다.
(B) 시체를 천으로 덮는다.
(C) 시체의 해골을 비운다.
(D) 시체를 무언가로 채운다.

정답 (A)

해설 미라를 만들 때는 뇌와 대부분의 장기를 꺼내고 내부에 톱밥이나 리넨 패드로 채우고, 방부제를 넣는다. 그런 후에 천으로 미라를 인간 모양의 관에 넣는다.

ORGANIZATION

a soul,
after death,
the brain and internal organs,
empty insides,
wrap it,
in a coffin

■ Exercise 2

컴퓨터 수업의 대화를 듣고 물음에 답하시오.

🎧 스크립트

P Hacking is when a person gains access to a computer system without authorization. Some of the major computer hacking that has been committed has been done by teenagers. For example, some Portuguese hackers once launched a political attack on the web page of the Indonesian government, focusing on that country's continued oppression of East Timor. The attack was online for about 3 hours at the web site of the Department of Foreign Affairs in the Republic of Indonesia. What do you think that the hackers did?

S Did they mess up the system and make it crash?

P No. Real hackers do not delete or destroy any information on the system that they hack. Hackers do what they do because they love the thrill of getting into a system that is supposedly unbreakable. The Portuguese hackers did not delete or change anything. They said, 'We just hack pages.'

교수 해킹이란 어떤 사람이 (사용) 인증 없이 컴퓨터 시스템에 접속하는 것을 말합니다. 지금까지 있었던 몇몇 주요 컴퓨터 해킹은 10대에 의해 발생하였습니다. 예를 들어, 포르투갈 해커 몇 명이 언젠가 동 티모르에 대한 계속된 억압에 초점을 두고, 인도네시아 정부의 웹 페이지에 정치적 공격을 가한 적이 있습니다. 그 공격은 인도네시아 공화국 외무부의 웹 사이트에 온라인 상으로 약 3시간 동안 행해졌습니다. 해커들이 무엇을 했을 거라고 생각하나요?

학생 시스템을 망가뜨리고 파괴했나요?

교수 아니요. 진짜 해커들은 자신이 해킹하고 있는 시스템의 어떤 정보도 삭제하거나 파괴하지 않습니다. 해커들이 해킹을 하는 이유는, 절대로 부수고 들어갈 수 없으리라 생각되는 시스템으로 들어가는 스릴을 즐기기 때문입니다. 이 포르투갈 해커들은 아무 것도 삭제하지 않았고 바꾸지도 않았습니다. 그들은 '우리는 그저 웹 페이지를 해킹할 뿐이다.'라고 말했습니다.

1 교수가 포르투갈인 해커에 대해 언급한 이유는 무엇인가?
(A) 유럽의 유명한 해커의 이름을 제시하려고
(B) 진짜 해커들과 그들이 하는 일을 예로 들려고
(C) (컴퓨터) 시스템에 들어갈 수 있는 가장 일반적인 방법을 설명하려고
(D) 해킹이 (컴퓨터) 시스템에 어떤 손상을 끼치는지 보여 주려고

정답 (B)

해설 해커들이 컴퓨터 시스템을 공격하는 이유는, 깰 수 없으리라 생각되는 시스템으로 들어가는 스릴을 즐기기 때문이다. 교수는 그런 해킹의 예로 포르투갈 해커의 해킹을 들고 있다.

2 교수에 따르면, 해킹이란 무엇인가?
(A) 매우 젊은 컴퓨터 프로그래머가 되는 것
(B) 정부의 승인 없이 컴퓨터 시스템을 바꾸는 것
(C) 컴퓨터 시스템 접속에 숙달되는 것
(D) 승인 없이 컴퓨터 시스템 안에 들어가는 것

정답 (D)

해설 해킹은 (사용) 인증 없이 컴퓨터 시스템에 들어가는 것이다.

ORGANIZATION
without authorization,
launch a political attack,
delete or destroy

■ Exercise **3**

사회 수업 시간의 토론을 듣고 물음에 답하시오.

🎧 스크립트

P In Britain, amongst certain people, fox hunting is a popular sport. Today we're going to discuss the issues surrounding fox hunting. What are your initial thoughts about this?

S1 The fox is a pest and its population needs to be controlled. Any concerned farmer would agree with this. Responsible fox management includes maintaining a healthy fox population without threatening livestock or other wildlife.

S2 But the official fox hunting season runs from November to April; yet fox cubs are usually born in March, which means that pregnant and nursing foxes are hunted and killed. Is this right?

S1 Foxes cause significant lamb, piglet, and poultry losses. Fox hunting is the most natural method of management. It removes the old, sick, and injured foxes. If it wasn't for fox hunting they would overpopulate and would eventually have to be caught and shot, or gassed.

교수 여우 사냥은 일부 영국 사람들 사이에서 인기 있는 오락거리입니다. 오늘 우리는 이 여우 사냥을 둘러싼 논쟁에 대해 토론할 것입니다. 이에 대해 처음으로 떠오르는 생각은 무엇입니까?

학생1 여우는 해로운 동물이기 때문에 그 개체수를 통제할 필요가 있습니다. 여우 때문에 걱정하고 있는 농부라면 누구라도 이 점에 동의할 겁니다. 책임 있는 여우 관리에는 가축이나 다른 야생동물을 위협하지 않고 건강한 여우 개체수를 유지하는 것이 포함됩니다.

학생2 그러나 공인된 여우 사냥 시즌은 11월에서 4월까지입니다. 하지만 여우 새끼는 주로 3월에 태어납니다. 이 말은 새끼를 배거나 젖을 먹이는 여우가 사냥 대상이 되어 죽는다는 뜻입니다. 이것이 타당한가요?

학생1 여우 때문에 새끼 양이나 새끼 돼지, 사육되고 있는 조류들이 심각할 정도로 줄어들고 있습니다. 여우 사냥은 가장 자연스러운 관리 수단입니다. 여우 사냥을 통해 늙고, 병들고, 부상당한 여우들을 제거할 수 있으니까요. 여우 사냥이 없다면 여우 개체수가 넘쳐나게 되니까, 결국 잡아서 사살하거나 가스로 질식시켜야 할 겁니다.

1 교수가 다음과 같이 말한 이유는 무엇인가?

🎧 **What are your initial thoughts about this?**

(A) 학생들이 수업에 참여할 수 있도록 격려하려고
(B) 학생들이 숙제를 했는지 물어보려고
(C) 대부분 사람들은 초기에 잘못된 생각을 한다는 것을 의미하려고
(D) 여우 사냥에 대한 일반적인 가설을 제시하려고

정답 (A)

해설 교수는 여우 사냥을 둘러싼 토론을 이끌어내기 위해 학생들의 참여를 유도하고 있다.

2 여자가 여우 사냥 시즌에 대해 언급한 이유는 무엇인가?

(A) 사람들이 일년 내내 사냥을 할 수 없다는 점을 지적하려고
(B) 여우 사냥이 매우 잔인한 오락거리라는 점을 지적하려고
(C) 사람들이 새끼를 배거나 젖을 먹이는 여우까지도 사냥하고 있다는 점을 지적하려고
(D) 새끼를 밴 여우를 죽이기가 너무 쉽다는 점을 지적하려고

정답 (C)

해설 공식적인 여우 사냥 시즌 안에 주로 새끼가 태어나는 달이 속해 있으므로, 새끼를 밴 여우가 희생당할 가능성이 있다는 점을 지적하고 있다.

ORGANIZATION

a pest,
without threatening,
the official fox hunting season,
pregnant and nursing foxes

■ Exercise4

두 학생 사이의 대화를 듣고 물음에 답하시오.

🎧 스크립트

S1 Oh, I wish we didn't have a field trip this weekend. I have so many things to do.
S2 Yeah, me too. I need to do some shopping. But I guess it can wait until next week. I'll see you there.
S1 Actually, I'm thinking of giving it a miss. I promised to help my friend do some painting. I don't think it will matter much if I'm not there.
S2 Really? You know… the professor strongly values attendance above all else.
S1 That's true! (Sigh…)
S2 I guess your friend will understand if you can't help her.
S1 Yeah, maybe. I'll give her a call later.
S2 Sounds like the sensible thing to do. See

you on the weekend then.
S1 Okay, see you. And thanks for the good advice.
S2 Anytime.

학생1 아, 이번 주에 견학 여행을 가지 않았으면 좋겠어. 할 일이 너무 많아.
학생2 응, 나도 그래. 쇼핑을 해야 하거든. 하지만 다음 주까지 미룰 수는 있을 거야. 거기서 보자.
학생1 사실, 빠질까 생각 중이야. 친구가 페인트 칠 하는 걸 도와주기로 약속했거든. 거기 가지 않는다고 그다지 문제되지 않을 것 같아.
학생2 정말? 하지만 너도 알다시피, 교수님은 다른 무엇보다도 출석에 큰 비중을 두시잖아.
학생1 맞는 말이야. (한숨)
학생2 네가 도와주지 못해라도 네 친구가 이해할 거야.
학생1 응, 아마 그러겠지. 친구에겐 나중에 전화해야겠어.
학생2 잘 생각한 거야. 그럼 주말에 보자.
학생1 그래, 안녕. 그리고 좋은 조언 해줘서 고마워.
학생2 언제든지.

1 여자가 다음과 같이 말한 이유는 무엇인가?

🎧 **You know… the professor strongly values attendance above all else.**

(A) 남자의 행동에 대해 불평하려고
(B) 견학 여행을 가야 한다고 남자를 설득하려고
(C) 교수가 마음이 다치지 않도록 보호하려고
(D) 남자가 대학 생활을 제대로 할 수 있도록 도우려고

정답 (B)

해설 교수님이 무엇보다 출석을 중요하게 생각한다는 점을 강조하면서 남자가 견학 여행을 빠지면 안 된다고 말한다.

2 남자는 다음에 무슨 일을 하겠는가?

(A) 페인트 칠을 한다.
(B) 쇼핑을 간다.
(C) 친구에게 전화한다.
(D) 교수에게 전화한다.

정답 (C)

해설 남자는 여자의 조언에 따라 견학 여행을 가기로 결정했다. 그러므로 친구에게 도와줄 수 없다고 전화할 것이다.

ORGANIZATION

this weekend,
promised to help his friend this weekend,
values attendance,
call his friend,
take the field trip

Dictation for Exercise

Exercise 1

① a preserved body
② would live on after death
③ for the passage into the afterlife
④ performed by
⑤ stuffing the empty insides with
⑥ wrapped the mummy
⑦ placed it
⑧ buried with them

✓ Check-up for Expression

1. performed by
   그 일은 로봇이 한 것이다.
2. be able to
   우리는 더 많은 수익을 낼 수 있을 것이다.
3. complicated procedures
   우리는 마감일을 지키려면 그 복잡한 절차를 보다 간소화할 필요가 있다.

Exercise 2

① gains access to
② has been committed
③ launched a political attack
④ online for about 3 hours
⑤ mess up
⑥ make it crash
⑦ that they hack
⑧ the thrill of
⑨ supposedly unbreakable
⑩ hack pages

✓ Check-up for Expression

1. messed up
   예기치 못한 결과로 그 프로젝트는 엉망이 되었다.
2. gain access to
   네트워크 정보에 접속하려면 사용자 이름과 비밀 번호를 넣으시오.
3. launched an attack
   그 조직은 정부에 대항하여 공격을 시작했다.

Exercise 3

① the issues surrounding
② What are your initial thoughts
③ needs to be controlled
④ without threatening
⑤ runs from
⑥ pregnant and nursing foxes
⑦ It removes
⑧ If it wasn't for
⑨ caught and shot

✓ Check-up for Expression

1. agree with
   그의 가설은 사실과 맞지 않는다.
2. are going to
   그들은 그 문제를 토론하는 데 많은 시간을 소비할 것이다.
3. method of
   그 학교는 새로운 교수 방법을 적용할 것이다.

Exercise 4

① wish we didn't have
② it can wait until
③ giving it a miss
④ it will matter much
⑤ above all else
⑥ I'll give her a call later
⑦ the sensible thing to do

✓ Check-up for Expression

1. doesn't matter if
   네가 그것을 고의로 했는지 아닌지는 중요하지 않다.
2. field trip
   나는 야외 학습 활동이 교육적이라고 생각하지 않는다.
3. attendance
   교수는 학생들의 출석률이 매우 낮아서 화가 났다.

Vocabulary Review

1. pilot	시험적인, 예비의
2. questionnaire	앙케이트, 질문서
3. conduct	(업무 등을) 수행[처리]하다
4. common	공통의, 보통의
5. available	이용할 수 있는, 쓸모있는
6. dilemma	진퇴양난, 딜레마
7. fix	고치다, 수정하다
8. sign	서명하다
9. submit	제출하다
10. resource	자원, 재원
11. prescription	처방(약)
12. correct	정정하다, 고치다
13. species	(생물) 종
14. warrant	보증하다, 장담하다
15. mummy	미라
16. initial	초기의, 처음의
17. experiment	실험
18. graduate	졸업하다
19. alter	바꾸다, 변경하다
20. abnormal	비정상의, 예외의
21. instruction	설명, 지시; 가르침
22. organism	유기체; 생물
23. accidentally	우연히
24. coffin	관

25. hacking   해킹
26. priest   성직자
27. nursing   양육 받는, 젖먹이의
28. poultry   가금(류)
29. procedure   절차, 진행
30. afterlife   사후, 내세
31. threaten   위협[협박]하다
32. livestock   가축(류)
33. overpopulate   인구 과잉으로 하다
34. internal organs   내장
35. field trip   (학생의) 실지 견학, 야외 연구 여행
36. stuff ~ with...   ~을 …로 채우다
37. gain access to ~   ~에 접근[출입]하다
38. give ~ a miss   빼먹다, 결석하다
39. launch an attack   공격을 개시하다
40. mess up   ~에 충격을 주다

FINAL TEST

■ Final Test 1

문학 수업의 강의를 듣고 물음에 답하시오.

🎧 스크립트

P Robert Browning has been considered to be the master of a form of poetry called the 'dramatic monologue.' He has had a great impact on modern poetry. The dramatic monologue, as we understand it today, is a lyric poem in which, during a dramatic moment in the speakers' life, they speak to a silent listener, the reader. We hear the dramatic monologue and sometimes get to understand the character of the speaker through what is said. The dramatic monologues of Robert Browning represent the most significant use of this form in post-romantic poetry. His monologues are characterized by certain easily identified features. The reader takes the role of the silent listener, the speaker in the poem argues, and the poems do not contain all the facts. Readers must decide for themselves the answers to any questions that they might have, therefore the poems are very interactive. The reader plays an active not a passive role.

교수 로버트 브라우닝은 '극적 독백'이라 불리는 시 형식의 대가로 간주되고 있습니다. 그는 현대 시에 엄청난 영향을 주고 있는데요, 우리가 오늘날 이해하는 것처럼, 극적 독백은 서정시의 하나로, 화자의 삶에 일어난 극적인 순간을 침묵하는 청취자인 독자에게 말하는 것입니다. 우리는 극적 독백을 듣고, 들은 내용을 통해 때로 화자의 성격을 이해하게 됩니다. 로버트 브라우닝의 극적 독백은 후기 낭만파 시에서 이 형식이 매우 중요하게 사용된 대표적인 예로 꼽힙니다. 그의 독백은 쉽게 식별되는 특징들을 가지고 있습니다. 독자는 침묵하는 청취자의 역할을 맡고, 시 속의 화자는 논쟁을 벌이고, 시는 모든 사실을 포함하지 않습니다. 독자는 자신이 갖게 될 어떤 질문에 대한 대답도 혼자 힘으로 판단해야만 합니다. 그러므로 시는 매우 상호작용적입니다. 독자는 수동적 역할이 아닌 능동적 역할을 담당하는 것이죠.

1 강의의 주된 내용은 무엇인가?

(A) 매우 유명한 시인
(B) 독자의 역할
(C) 청취자의 역할
(D) 특정한 시 형식

정답 (D)

해설 교수는 '극적 독백'이라는 시 형식을 설명하면서 로버트 브라우닝의 작법 형태를 예로 들고 있다.

2 교수는 로버트 브라우닝에 대해 무엇이라 말하는가?

(A) 그는 극적 독백이라는 현대 시를 창안했다.
(B) 그는 위대한 드라마 작가이기도 했다.
(C) 그는 이런 스타일의 시를 낭송하는 데 탁월했다.
(D) 그는 현대 시에 커다란 영향을 미쳤다.

정답 (D)

해설 로버트 브라우닝은 '극적 독백'이라는 현대 시에 지대한 영향을 미치며 이러한 시 기법의 대가로 인정받고 있다. 드라마를 쓴다거나 이 시의 창안자라는 언급은 없다.

3 교수에 따르면, 다음 중 로버트 브라우닝의 독백이 가진 특징이 아닌 것은?

(A) 독자는 침묵의 청취자 역할을 담당한다.
(B) 독자는 더욱 광범위한 이야기를 결정한다.
(C) 독자는 대중 앞에서 화자와 논쟁한다.
(D) 독자와 화자가 시에 영향을 미친다.

정답 (C)

해설 극적 독백의 특징은 강의의 뒷부분에 자세하게 설명되어 있다. 독자는 침묵의 청취자이고, 논쟁을 벌이는 것은 시 속의 화자이다. 시는 모든 사실을 포함하지 않아 독자가 스스로 결정해야 한다. 그러므로 시에서 독자와 화자는 서로 의사소통 하는 능동적 역할을 담당한다.

4 교수는 어떤 방식으로 극적 독백에 대해 설명하는가?

(A) 극적 독백을 쓰는 방법을 보여줌으로써
(B) 브라우닝의 시작 스타일을 분석함으로써
(C) 몇몇 작품을 예로 듦으로써
(D) 이를 현대 시와 비교함으로써

정답 (B)

해설 브라우닝의 시에 나타나는 두드러진 특징을 나열함으로써 극적 독백을 설명한다.

■ Final Test 2

학생과 행정 직원의 대화를 듣고 물음에 답하시오.

🎧 스크립트

S Excuse me. I was wondering what the meal plan is at the cafeteria this term.
A Well, there are three options this term, so you can choose.

S Oh, that's good. I don't eat much so I usually end up paying for more than I eat!
A And I usually still feel hungry after eating. That is one reason why we decided to change the system.
S So what are the options?
A You can pay $10 per day for the main meal, the starter, and the dessert. That's option one. Oh! That's one of the changes. They are offering a starter now; soup, bread or something.
S I see. But I don't think I'll need a starter.
A Okay! So, option two is $8 per day for the main meal and the dessert. Option three is just $5 for the main meal. Which plan do you think you'll be going for?
S I think I'll go for option three.
A Three it is then. I'll get the form for you.

학생 실례합니다. 이번 학기 카페테리아 식단에 대해 알고 싶은데요.
직원 음, 이번 학기에는 선택사항이 세 가지 있어서 그 중에서 선택할 수 있어요.
학생 아, 잘 됐네요. 저는 그다지 많이 먹는 편이 아니어서 언제나 먹는 것에 비해 식비를 많이 지불하는 편이거든요.
직원 저는 먹고 난 후에도 여전히 허기가 지는데. 그게 우리가 체계를 바꾸기로 한 한 가지 이유죠.
학생 그러면 선택사항으로는 어떤 것이 있나요?
직원 메인 요리와, 애피타이저, 디저트를 합해서 하루에 10달러를 지불하는 게 있습니다. 그것이 선택사항 1번이죠. 아, 한 가지 바뀐 것이 있어요. 에피타이저로 스프나 빵, 또는 기타 음식이 제공됩니다.
학생 알겠어요. 하지만 저는 애피타이저가 필요 없을 것 같아요.
직원 좋아요. 그러면, 선택 2번이 있어요. 이것은 메인 요리와 디저트를 포함해서 하루에 8달러예요. 선택 3번은 메인 요리만 제공하고 단 5달러지요. 어떤 것을 선택할 생각인가요?
학생 저는 3번을 선택하겠어요.
직원 네, 3번이라고요. 신청서를 가져다 줄게요.

1 여자가 남자를 찾아간 이유는 무엇인가?

(A) 점심식사비를 지불하려고
(B) 저녁 식사하러 함께 나가자고 요청하려고
(C) 이번 학기의 식사 계획은 어떤지 물어보려고
(D) 학교 식단에 대해 불평하려고

정답 (C)

해설 여자는 이번 학기 식단에 대해 알고 싶어 행정직원을 찾아갔다.

2 대화에 따르면, 다음 중 사실인 것은? 정답 두 개를 고르시오.

(A) 선택사항1은 디저트를 포함하지만, 선택사항 3은 포함하지 않는다.
(B) 선택사항 2는 디저트와 애피타이저를 제공한다.
(C) 선택사항 1은 디저트를 포함하지만, 선택사항 2는 포함하지 않는다.
(D) 선택사항 3은 메인 요리를 포함하지만, 애피타이저나 디저트는 포함하지 않는다.

정답 (A) (D)

해설 선택사항 1 = 애피타이저 + 메인 요리 + 디저트
선택사항 2 = 메인 요리 + 디저트
선택사항 3 = 메인 요리

3 대화 일부를 다시 들으시오.

🎧 And I usually still feel hungry after eating. That is one reason why we decided to change the system.

남자가 다음과 같이 말할 때 그 의미는 무엇인가?

🎧 That is one reason why we decided to change the system.

(A) 음식의 질이 그다지 좋지 않았다.
(B) 학생들에게 식사량이 충분하지 않다.
(C) 학생들이 식사비로 너무 많이 지불해왔다.
(D) 새 식단은 학생 각자의 식사량에 맞추기 위해 고안되었다.

정답 (D)

해설 학생 개개인에 따라 식사량이 다르기 때문에 식사를 선택할 수 있도록 식단 체제를 바꾼 것이다.

4 여자는 다음으로 무슨 일을 할 것인가?

(A) 카페테리아에 간다.
(B) 신청서를 작성한다.
(C) 선택사항을 선택한다.
(D) 식사대금을 지불한다.

정답 (B)

해설 선택사항 3을 선택하기로 결정했으므로, 행정직원이 가져다 주는 신청서 양식을 작성할 것이다.

■ Final Test 3

인류학 수업의 강의를 듣고 물음에 답하시오.

🎧 스크립트

P The Blackfoot Indians were well-known for their expert horsemanship and great skills in hunting buffalo. They had a reputation as warriors and fought fiercely for their territory. By the end of the 19th century, the population of Blackfoot Indians declined due to a combination of the effects of numerous diseases on the tribes and the near extinction of their main resource, the buffalo. The Blackfoot Indians were nomadic hunter gatherers who lived in tepees, which is a round tent made from animal skins or outer covering of trees. And they subsisted mainly on herds of buffalo using them for food. Actually the Blackfoot Indians used all of the buffalo that they killed; using the bones for tools, hide for clothing, and the hooves to make glue. Now, let's move on to the roles of men and women. As you may guess, men had the prime responsibilities of hunting and war. On the other hand, the women made tepees, meals, weapons, shields, tools, drums, and pipes. Both these roles were instrumental in the functioning of their society.

교수 블랙풋 인디언들은 노련하게 말을 타고, 들소(버팔로) 사냥에 뛰어난 기술을 발휘하는 것으로 유명했습니다. 그들은 전사로서의 명성을 구축했고, 그들의 영토를 지키기 위해 맹렬하게 싸웠습니다. 19세기 말, 블랙풋 인디언의 인구는, 이 부족에게 닥친 수많은 질병으로 인해, 또한 그들의 주요 자원인 들소가 거의 멸종 지경에 이르면서 감소했습니다. 블랙풋 인디언들은 유목 생활을 하는 사냥꾼이자 채취자로, 동물 가죽이나 나무의 외피로 덮은 둥근 텐트인 티피에서 살았습니다. 그리고 주로 들소들을 식량으로 사용하며 이들에 의존해 생활했습니다. 사실, 블랙풋 인디언은 들소를 잡아 그들의 모든 부위를 사용하지요. 뼈로는 도구를 만들었고, 가죽으로는 옷을 만들었고, 발굽으로는 풀을 만들었습니다. 자, 이제 남성과 여성의 역할에 대해 말해봅시다. 여러분이 추측하듯이 남성은 사냥과 전쟁을 주로 책임졌습니다. 반면에 여성은 티피를 만들고, 식사를 준비하고, 무기와 방패, 도구, 북, 파이프 등을 만들었습니다. 둘 다 사회가 기능하는 데 도구적 역할이었습니다.

1 강의의 주된 내용은 무엇인가?

(A) 블랙풋 인디언의 난폭성
(B) 블랙풋 인디언의 사냥 방법
(C) 블랙풋 인디언으로부터의 위험
(D) 블랙풋 인디언의 생활

정답 (D)

해설 유목민으로서 수렵과 농경 생활을 했던 블랙풋 인디언의 생활을 실례를 들어 자세하게 설명하고 있다.

2 블랙풋 인디언의 인구가 감소한 주요 원인은 무엇인가? 정답 두 개를 고르시오.

(A) 그들이 병에 걸렸기 때문에
(B) 기후가 급격히 변했기 때문에
(C) 들소 수가 감소했기 때문에
(D) 티피에서 살았기 때문에

정답 (A) (C)

해설 강의에 따르면 블랙풋 인디언의 인구감소 원인은 첫째, 종족에게 덮친 수많은 질병, 둘째, 그들의 주요 자원인 들소 수의 급격한 감소, 두 가지이다. 기후 변화에 대한 언급은 없다.

3 교수에 따르면, 블랙풋 인디언은 들소를 어떻게 사용했는가? 정답 세 개를 고르시오.

(A) 유용한 도구를 만들기 위해
(B) 입을 옷을 만들기 위해
(C) 무기를 만들기 위해
(D) 돈으로 사용하기 위해

정답 (A) (B) (C)

해설 블랙풋 인디언은 들소의 모든 부위를 사용했던 것으로 유명하다. 뼈로는 도구를 만들었고, 가죽으로는 옷을 만들었고, 발굽으로는 풀을 만들었다.

4 교수에 따르면, 다음 중 블랙풋 인디언에 대해 사실인 것은?

(A) 남자들은 자신의 은신처를 짓는 데 뛰어난 기술을 가졌다.
(B) 여자들은 무기나 도구의 제작을 담당했다.
(C) 그들은 질병에 걸리지 않았다.
(D) 그들은 주로 식물이나 물고기를 먹고 살았다.

정답 (B)

해설 (A) 집을 짓는 것은 여자들의 몫이었다. (C) 수많은 질병으로 블랙풋 인디언의 숫자가 감소했다. (D) 그들의 주 식량원은 들소였다.

■ Final Test 4

심리학 수업의 대화를 듣고 물음에 답하시오.

🎧 스크립트

P A phobia is an irrational and persistent fear of objects or situations. Phobias are more common than you might think, and often involve a fear of ordinary things that does not appear to have any physical explanation, such as a fear of frogs! People suffering from phobias display anxieties that often interfere with normal routines. There are three main categories of phobias: simple, social, and agoraphobia. Simple phobias are an extreme fear of specific objects; while social phobias are a fear of being embarrassed or scrutinized in a social environment, such as public speaking. Agoraphobia, however, is the intense fear of being in large or busy places, where people are afraid of having a panic attack. Agoraphobia is, in fact, a fear of fear. Now, is anyone here afraid of anything, anything unusual?

S I'm scared of spiders.

P That's quite common, there are many more unusual fears. For example if you have hippopotomonstrosesquippedaliophobia, you will be feeling rather uncomfortable right now, because that's a fear of long words! Phobias are not easily explained, and their causes are hotly debated.

교수 공포증은 물체나 상황에 대한 불합리하고 지속적인 두려움입니다. 공포증은 여러분이 생각하는 것보다 더 흔합니다. 또한 어떤 물리적인 이유도 없어 보이는 평범한 것에 대한 공포를 포함하는 경우도 종종 있습니다. 개구리에 대한 공포처럼 말입니다. 공포증을 겪는 사람들은 종종 정상적인 일과를 방해하는 불안감을 나타냅니다. 공포증에는 단순 공포증, 사회 공포증, 광장 공포증 등 세 가지 주요 범주가 있습니다. 단순 공포증은 특정한 물체에 대한 극도의 공포입니다. 반면에 사회 공포증은 사회 속에서 당황하거나 사람들 앞에서 자신의 모습이 속속들이 파헤쳐지는 데 대한 공포입니다. 많은 사람들 앞에서 말을 해야 하는 것과 같은 경우가 그것입니다. 그러나 광장 공포증은 넓고 혼잡한 장소에 있는 데 대한 강렬한 공포입니다. 이런 장소에서 사람들은 공황 발작을 겪게 될까 두려워합니다. 사실, 광장 공포증은 공포 자체에 대한 공포라 할 수 있습니다. 자, 여기 여러분 중에 어떤 것, 특이한 어떤 것을 두려워하는 사람이 있나요?

학생 전 거미를 무서워합니다.

교수 그건 아주 흔한 현상이에요. 그보다 더 유별난 공포도 많아요. 예를 들어, 히포포토몬스트로지스큅달리오포비아(hippopotomonstrosesquippedaliophobia, 긴 단어에 대한 공포증)를 가지고 있다면, 여러분은 지금 불안함을 느낄 거예요. 이것은 긴 단어에 대한 공포거든요. 공포증은 쉽게 설명되지도 않을 뿐 아니라, 공포증의 원인은 뜨거운 논쟁거리입니다.

1 강의의 주된 내용은 무엇인가?

(A) 합리적이지 않은 공포
(B) 일반적이거나 특이한 공포들
(C) 세 가지 심리적 문제
(D) 공포증과 그 원인

정답 (D)

해설 강의 내용은 공포증의 정의와 종류, 특이한 공포증의 예 등으로 구성되어 있다.

2 다음 각 설명과 일치하는 곳에 체크하시오.

	단순 공포증	사회 공포증	광장 공포증
개구리나 거미와 같은 것에 대한 공포	✔		
넓고 혼잡한 장소에 있는 데 대한 공포			✔
특정 물체에 대한 극도의 공포	✔		
사람들과 있을 때 느끼는 당혹감		✔	
공황 발작을 일으키는 것에 대한 두려움			✔
대중들 앞에서 말하는 데 대한 공포		✔	

해설 단순 공포증은 특정한 물체에 대한 극도의 공포이다. 사회 공포증은 사람들 앞에서 말하는 것처럼 사회 환경 속에서 당황하거나 자신의 모습이 속속들이 파헤쳐지는 데 대한 공포이다. 광장 공포증은 커다랗거나 혼잡한 장소에 있는 데 대한 강렬한 공포이다. 이런 공포증을 가진 사람들은 공황 발작을 겪을까 봐 두려워한다.

3 교수가 hippopotomonstrosesquippedaliophobia에 대해 언급한 이유는 무엇인가?
(A) 긴 단어를 말하는 자신의 솜씨를 과시하려고
(B) 학생들이 귀담아 듣고 있는지 점검하려고
(C) 강의를 재미있고 기억하기 쉽게 만들려고
(D) 특이한 공포증의 한 예를 들려고

정답 (D)

해설 공포증 중에는 매우 특이한 공포증이 있다고 말하면서, 긴 단어에 대한 공포증을 그 예로 들었다.

4 강의의 일부를 다시 들으시오.

🎧 Agoraphobia, however, is the intense fear of being in large or bsy places, where people are afraid of having a panic attack. Agoraphobia is, in fact, a fear of fear.

교수가 다음과 같이 말할 때 그 말이 의미하는 것은?

🎧 Agoraphobia is, in fact, a fear of fear.
(A) 광장 공포증은 공포의 구체적인 대상이 없다.
(B) 광장 공포증은 쉽게 설명된다.
(C) 광장 공포증은 전혀 공포가 아니다.
(D) 광장 공포증은 다른 공포증과 구별되는 특별한 특징이 없다.

정답 (A)

해설 광장 공포증은 공황 발작을 겪게 될까 두려워하는 증상이므로 공포의 구체적인 대상이 없는 공포에 대한 공포이다.

넥서스 중등 영어 시리즈

Reading 시리즈

Reading 공감
Level 1~3

After School Reading
Level 1~3

THIS IS READING
1~4
전면 개정판

Smart Reading Basic
Level 1~2
Smart Reading
Level 1~2

Listening 시리즈

Listening 공감
Level 1~3

After School Listening
Level 1~3

The Listening
Level 1~4

도전! 만점 중학 영어듣기 모의고사
Level 1~3

공든탑 Listening
유형편, 적용편
실전모의고사 1·2

리스닝 본능
Level 1~4

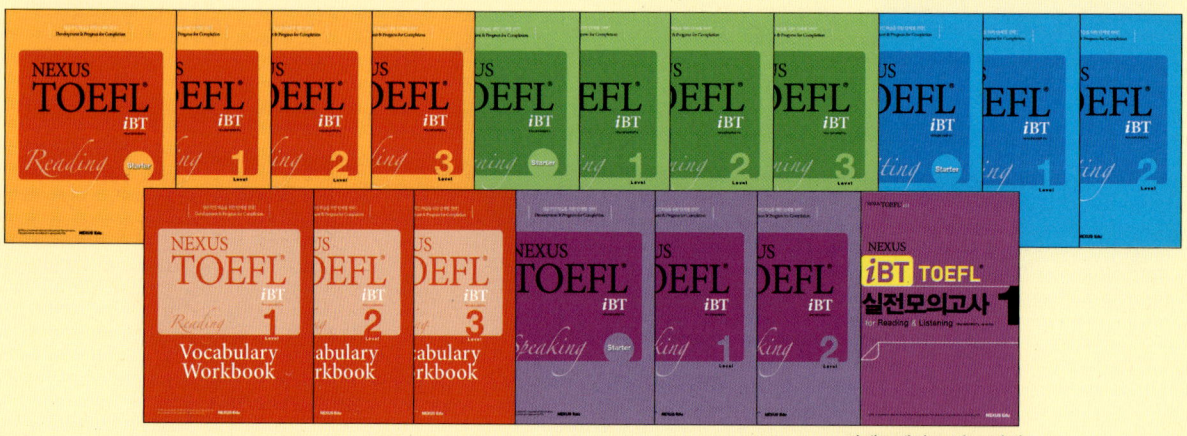